Rosemary Auchmuty was ~~born~~ ... American mother and an Irish ~~father~~. ~~She g~~... Australia, and was educated at Newcastle Girls' High School (where she was school captain) and the Australian National University, from which she obtained a Ph.D. in history in 1975. She has lived in London since 1978. After several years teaching history and women's studies in adult and higher education, she took up the study of law part-time as a mature student, and is now Chair of the Department of Academic Legal Studies at the University of Westminster. She has published several short stories, two school textbooks, and many articles on women's history and feminist legal studies. Her first study of girls' school stories was *A World of Girls: The Appeal of the Girls' School Story* (The Women's Press, 1992).

Rosemary Auchmuty has been an avid reader of stories about British girls' boarding schools since she was nine years old, probably because she did not go to one.

A WORLD OF WOMEN
Growing up in the Girls' School Story
ROSEMARY AUCHMUTY

First published by The Women's Press Ltd, 1999
A member of the Namara Group
34 Great Sutton Street, London EC1V 0LQ

British Library Cataloguing-in-Publication Data
A catalogue record for this book is available from the British Library.

ISBN 0 7043 4538 2

Typeset in Bembo 11/13pt by FSH Ltd, London
Printed and bound in Great Britain by Cox & Wyman Ltd, Reading, Berkshire

To all my friends among the members of

The New Chalet Club
The Elsie Jeanette Oxenham Appreciation Society
The Dorita Fairlie Bruce Society
and
The Friends of the Chalet School

who have been so generous with their books, knowledge,
ideas, and fellowship

Contents

Acknowledgements

My greatest debt in writing this book has been to the communities of school-story enthusiasts, of whose existence I was unaware when I published *A World of Girls* in 1992. The book had scarcely appeared before I was contacted by representatives of the various appreciation societies and fanzines dedicated to girls' school stories, whose ranks I swiftly joined. The centenary celebrations for Elinor Brent-Dyer in 1994 provided a rallying point for Chalet fans and brought me into personal contact with dozens – indeed, hundreds – of people whose experience of school stories, while not identical to my own, was equally important for *them*. It is no exaggeration to say that, through the appreciation societies, I encountered an entire new social circle. I also made the expensive acquaintance of the specialist dealers who feed our addiction, but who are also friends, sharing knowledge as well as finding books for us.

Through all these networks I have enjoyed discussions both serious and light-hearted about practically every aspect of the books of Elsie Oxenham, Dorita Fairlie Bruce, Elinor Brent-Dyer and many other authors for girls. With them I have retraced the steps of the Chalet girls in Hereford, Austria and Switzerland, and of the Abbey girls in Sussex, the Chilterns and at Cleeve Abbey.

Among these new friends are many of the authorities in the field, upon whose work I had respectfully drawn in *A World of Girls*: people like Mary Cadogan, whose brilliant pioneering studies of girls' fiction and other popular literary genres demonstrate a staggering breadth of expertise;[1] Sheila Ray, whose *The Blyton Phenomenon* (1982) was the first book to give serious critical attention to a despised popular children's author;[2] and Helen McClelland and Monica Godfrey, biographers of Elinor Brent-Dyer and Elsie Oxenham respectively.[3] All have been, and continue to be, exceptionally generous with their expertise. But there are also many others in the appreciation societies who have not only enhanced my own understanding of the books but done as much to advance knowledge in the field as any academic study. For although children's literature has become a 'respectable' area of scholarship in university circles over the last decade or so, in marked contrast to earlier years when interest was largely confined to the less prestigious publications of librarians and teachers, girls' school stories have been slow to achieve anything like an accurate assessment of their worth or, indeed, an accurate appraisal at all. General accounts tend to be dismissive, niggardly and error-prone.[4] Caricature is still never far away, and girls' school stories continue to be reproached for lack of realism and the absence of boy–girl relationships.[5] They are frequently ignored altogether: recent work by P. W. Musgrave, Dennis Butts and Jeffrey Richards on 'the school story' turns out to be about boys' school stories only.[6] There is no doubt in my mind that a prime cause of this neglect and misrepresentation is the fact that girls' school stories depict a world of girls and women, a subject which has never enjoyed high status in the eyes of patriarchal scholarship.

Since the publication of *A World of Girls*, the situation has certainly improved. Sheila Ray's entry on school stories in the *International Companion Encyclopedia of Children's Literature* accords girls' school stories an accurate, sympathetic hearing.[7] A surprising number of recent masters and doctoral theses have taken girls' school stories as their subject matter, and relevant articles are becoming more common in the academic journals. Nicholas Tucker and Kimberley Reynolds of the National Centre for Research in Children's Literature's 1998 conference on the school story gave a plenary slot to the girls' version of the genre.[8] The forthcoming second volume of

Encyclopaedia of School Stories, devoted to girls' school stories, is substantially larger than the one devoted to boys', and will go a long way towards setting the record straight.[9]

The change of critical climate is due to the combined efforts of the girls' school-story enthusiasts, who, in bravely proclaiming their enjoyment of the books, have enabled many other fans (men as well as women, and boys as well as girls) to come out of their closets and join their ranks, and of feminist scholars, who have made the study of women's culture acceptable in the academy. Brent-Dyer's biographer, Helen McClelland, recalls:

> In the 1970s it had seemed vital to write Elinor Brent-Dyer's story from a detached, even critical viewpoint; and with the expectation of socially conscious editors in mind I had deliberately highlighted for discussion the weaknesses of the books, being aware that anything enthusiastic would be instantly rejected.[10]

By the time she came to write *Elinor Brent-Dyer's Chalet School* in the late 1980s, this coolly distanced approach was no longer necessary. Likewise, the second edition of her biography, *Behind the Chalet School* (1996), differs from the first in more ways than the simple addition of new material; whole sections have been rewritten to provide a more positive assessment which is an accurate reflection of McClelland's own views.

Meanwhile, feminist scholarship had, by the mid-1990s, made possible an enterprise like that of Shirley Foster and Judy Simons, who, in examining Angela Brazil's *The Madcap of the School* alongside other 'classics' of girls' fiction, point out that 'girls' fiction prioritises feminine experience and consequently (whether implicitly or explicitly) explores the possibilities of female self-expression and fulfilment in a male-dominated world'.[11]

A World of Women owes its existence and its analysis to both these influences. As a feminist scholar myself, I must acknowledge the role of The Women's Press in providing a forum for feminist writing for more than twenty years in the face of considerable anti-feminist reaction, and when other small political publishers have gone under or sold out. I am particularly grateful to the Press's joint managing director, Kathy Gale, who commissioned this book, and to my editor, Kirsty Dunseath, who did her work not only with skill and competence (one expects that), but also with great sympathy and respect for the book's subject matter.

I would also like to thank Martina A. Greaves and HarperCollins Publishers for allowing me to reproduce quotations from the works of Elinor M. Brent-Dyer; John Bruce and the executors of the estate of Dorita Fairlie Bruce for permission to reproduce quotations from the works of Dorita Fairlie Bruce; and Desmond and Wendy Dunkerley for permission to reproduce quotations from the works of Elsie J. Oxenham. Thanks too to Joy Wotton, the editor of the *New Chalet Club Journal*, for allowing me to reprint in revised form some of the material in Chapter 5 and to quote from other people's contributions to that journal, as well as her own; Stella Waring, the editor of *Serendipity* (the Dorita Fairlie Bruce journal), for permission to quote from contributions to that journal, and from her own co-authored book (with Sheila Ray) *EJO: Her Work*; Ruth Allen, editor of the *Abbey Chronicle*, the journal of the Elsie J. Oxenham Appreciation Society, for bibliographical assistance; and Shereen Benjamin, Dennis Bird, Jill Ekersley, Doreen Litchfield, Helen McClelland, Sheila Ray, Martin Spence, Anne Thompson and Kate Tyler for permission to quote from their contributions to the *Chaletian*, the New Chalet Club *Journal*, *Serendipity* and *Folly*.

Sections of the book were presented in workshop form at the New Chalet Club's conferences in London in 1994 and 1995, organised in conjunction with Bettany Press; at the first

Annual General Meeting of the New Chalet Club in South Shields in 1996; at Stella Waring's WEA Study Day in Loughborough in 1996; and at the New Chalet Club's conference in Birmingham in 1997. I am grateful for the feedback, critique and ideas generated by my listeners at these sessions, and also that which has arisen through correspondence from customers of Bettany Press, founded by Ju Gosling and myself in 1994 to desktop-publish books of interest to girls'-school-story fans. From books, Ju moved on to film and electronic publishing, bringing the school-story debates to thousands around the world. Her knowledge, encouragement and enthusiasm have been an inspiration to many. My co-editors on the girls' volume of the *Encyclopaedia of School Stories*, Hilary Clare, Sue Sims and Joy Wotton, have taught me more than I knew existed about the full range of the genre and its writers.

Finally, thanks are due to my Head of School and colleagues at the University of Westminster for tolerating research interests which are not much help to a law school; and to my partner, Sibyl Grundberg, for mustering interest in an enthusiasm she finds impossible to share.

Rosemary Auchmuty
London, November 1998

A WORLD OF WOMEN

Introduction

Girls' school stories are not solely concerned with jolly japes in the dorm or hothouse emotions played out on the hockey field, as their detractors would have us believe. They are essentially tales about growing up, about learning to live in a community and preparing for womanhood. Serious lessons are to be gleaned from school stories; serious role models and ways of behaving are presented, for the genre is intrinsically educative. As Beverly Lyon Clark puts it, 'School stories lend themselves to didacticism because they are about schooling.'[1] Children's literature has always had a dual motivation – to entertain and to instruct – and the notion that books should provide a positive moral influence has been a powerful impetus behind even the most commercial literary production for the children's market, although ideas about what constitutes morality have differed from generation to generation.[2]

Girls' school stories are not, moreover, solely concerned with young people. Though girls are usually the central focus, a range of grown-up characters of greater or lesser significance generally forms part of the schoolgirls' world: the staff, of course; parents; Old Girls; other friends and mentors – often quite a mixed bag. With school-story series the possibilities are multiplied, for heroines actually grow up across the successive volumes – unlike the Famous Five or Anthony Buckeridge's schoolboy hero Jennings, who never get any older through two dozen books or more. Where would the Chalet School be without Jo Maynard? Jo ceases to be a schoolgirl in the eleventh book in the series but remains a vitally important character, on stage or off, for the remaining 48. Publishers sometimes balked at carrying a series past the heroine's schooldays,[3] and authors sometimes abandoned them in the sixth form,[4] but the heroines of the three great exponents of the girls' school story – Elsie J. Oxenham, Dorita Fairlie Bruce and Elinor M. Brent-Dyer – skilfully made the transition to womanhood, and readers continued to enjoy reading about them as working women, wives and mothers. The result is that a sizeable proportion of the novels in girls' school-story series are not primarily school stories at all. They are about school-story heroines, grown-up.

Focusing on growing up and grown-ups allows us to study the less commonly discussed non-school stories of the school-story writers. The series books which cover the growing-up stage of the former schoolgirl's life and those which portray her as an adult are, paradoxically, often very popular with school-story fans. A contributor to the *Chaletian* in 1994 cited *Jo to the Rescue*, which depicts Jo as a young mother on holiday in wartime with her three married women friends and all their children, as her favourite Chalet book.[5] Some writers for children – Enid Blyton and Arthur Ransome, to name but two – made a habit of removing all the adults by about the second chapter, in the belief that children do not want to read about grown-ups. But Dennis Bird, writing in *Serendipity*, recounts how, as a teenage boy in 1944, he came across Dorita Fairlie Bruce's *Nancy Calls the Tune* in a shop and recognised the title from other Nancy books he had borrowed from his sister:

> I found that here was something different from a girl's school story; here was Nancy Caird and her schoolfriends grown up, and what was more, involved in the Great War, which at that time – the D-Day year – was in the forefront of all her [sic] thoughts. My pocket money would just about run to the five shillings marked on the wrapper – so I bought it. I have never regretted it . . .[6]

2

In the school stories themselves, many readers love the chapters set in the staff room where the mistresses talk over school events at their leisure – a favourite device of Elinor Brent-Dyer, who uses it in nearly every book. Listening in to their conversations, 'Readers learn that the Chalet staff are human,' suggests Polly Goerres, 'and the child reader also learns that grown-ups too are human ...'[7]

Herein lies the rationale for *A World of Women*. In one sense this book is a sequel to *A World of Girls*, published in 1992, which argued that the appeal of the girls' school story for generations of girls and women lay in its depiction of an all-female world in which all things were possible – power, athletic and scholastic success, centrally important same-sex friendships and even same-sex love. In this world girls were relatively free to negotiate an identity and relationships outside patriarchal constraints, in contrast to their situation in real life. *A World of Girls* focused mainly, though not exclusively, on girls and young women. It dealt largely with the school setting and was less concerned with the many novels of the school-story writers which moved beyond the world of school into the home, the community, the workplace or on holiday: *Dimsie Grows Up, The Abbey Girls at Home* or *Jo to the Rescue*, for example. In these books school-story heroines leave school, take jobs, get married, become mothers, or simply spend time in the company of other adults. But the link with the school is never entirely broken: Dimsie's first job takes her back to her old school;[8] the Abbey girls remain members of *their* school's Hamlet Club; Jo haunts the Chalet School like a restless ghost (and indeed is frequently described as the 'spirit' of the place); and daughters and nieces forge even more powerful connections when they in turn are old enough to become pupils.

A World of Women examines the growing-up processes of the school-story heroines and the grown-up role models which are offered to readers. It looks at young and older single women; at the depictions of heterosexual romance, marriage and motherhood; at the wider female community of the books; and at careers which, barely contemplated for our wealthier heroines in the earlier books, had become *de rigueur* by the 1940s, in line with historical trends. The book argues that, despite steadily increasing pressures on young women to put their energies into relationships with men and family life, girls' school stories from the 1920s to the 1960s remained essentially a world of women, with even grown-up characters inhabiting largely all-female communities in which they could forge roles and relationships which prioritised themselves and other women rather than men.

Of course, men are often present – the great majority of school-story heroines marry, and one can hardly have a heterosexual romance without a man – and sometimes their patriarchal authority is heavy indeed, a classic instance being Dr Jack Maynard's habit of dropping a tranquilliser or two into his wife's coffee every time she seems a little stressed.[9] Nevertheless, considering the tenor of the times and the tone of contemporaneous literature (the romantic novel, for example), school stories offer a remarkable variety of independent, self-directed role models of single and married women supported by and supporting women friends in clubs, at home and at work, and mentoring younger women at school or in girls' organisations such as Guides, Guildry or Camp Fire. Thus were their ideals passed on in the story, and from story to reader.

In *A World of Girls* I examined the novels of Elsie J. Oxenham, Dorita Fairlie Bruce, Elinor M. Brent-Dyer and Enid Blyton. In *A World of Women* I have restricted myself to the first three, for Enid Blyton never wrote a 'growing-up' story; indeed, her eighteen-year-old sixth formers in the last Malory Towers book are the oldest heroines she ever portrayed.

Oxenham, Bruce and Brent-Dyer are by common consent the three 'greats' of the girls' school story. Each has her devoted following, and associated societies and magazines,[10] and many enthusiasts, myself included, love all three. They are great because they were prolific, professional and, at their best, very good writers. Among *cognoscenti* they are also the best-known girls' school-story writers, though Enid Blyton and Angela Brazil are perhaps more closely identified with the genre in the world at large, and this is mainly because they wrote series. Indeed, these three authors pioneered the school-story series in Britain. It was the series format which, more than anything else, ensured enduring popularity for their books when others, whose work was equally proficient, have faded from view.

The idea of the series was not new in the 1920s, but it was much more common in North America than in Britain.[11] Elsie Oxenham (1880–1960) can probably claim the credit for the first school-story series here, though when she published *The Abbey Girls* in 1920, featuring the same school as that of *The Girls of the Hamlet Club* (1914), she could hardly have imagined she was initiating a new phenomenon, or have foreseen that nearly 40 more Abbey titles would follow. Hard on her heels came Dorita Fairlie Bruce (1885–1970), whose first novel, *The Senior Prefect*, also appeared in 1920 (or possibly 1921). Quick to grasp the marketing possibilities of a series about the same heroine, her publishers (Oxford University Press) almost immediately retitled it *Dimsie Goes to School*. *Dimsie Moves Up*, *Dimsie Moves Up Again* and *Dimsie Among the Prefects* promptly followed. With *Dimsie Grows Up* (1924), Bruce continued Dimsie's story past her schooldays and up to her engagement. Oxenham had already done this with two of her heroines at the Abbey *Girls Go Back to School* (1922).

Both Oxenham and Bruce wrote a number of other school-story series during the 1920s and 1930s. Bruce may be considered the archetypal series writer: she wrote five different school-story series (and another non-school set), and not only can all her novels be attached to a series, but many of her short stories too.[12] Some of the settings and the characters overlap the various series, a phenomenon that was even truer of

Oxenham's work, which represents a vast web of inter-connecting life stories. But the person whose name is synonymous with the modern girls' school story, the author who laid down the 'one-book-one-term' paradigm which came to seem so characteristic of the school-series format, was Elinor Mary Brent-Dyer (1894–1969), author of the 59-strong Chalet series and many other girls' school stories. Brent-Dyer is the only one of the three whose books are still in print – and selling strongly.

As a marketing device the series was incomparable. After reading one story readers often became so interested in the characters they felt they had to find out what happened next (or, if they started in the middle of the series, what had gone before). So they would borrow other books in the series from friends or from the library and, like newly-weds matching household china, issue firm instructions to relatives for birthday and Christmas lists. Many of my own Abbey and Chalet books bear birthday inscriptions from my childhood years. The more we read, the more we yearned for the next instalment.[13]

But, more important than any commercial advantages, the series format gave writers licence to construct entire social worlds peopled with characters whom their readers came to know and love almost as if they were real. 'What draws me back to the Chalet School is the sense of recognition, the familiarity of the world portrayed by Elinor Brent-Dyer,' wrote one fan;

> ... how well one remembers the inky fingers and untidy hair of Jo and the starchy efficiency of Matey, brisk but sympathetic. The quiet Sundays, the fruitful Hobby periods ... are there to draw you into a secure and familiar community.[14]

In this world of girls and women, we readers could and can still lose ourselves, escaping from the real world with its patriarchal pressures, but also reinforcing our own sense of self, enriching our experience, and opening us up to new ideas and ways of being.

A World of Women also provides an opportunity to examine the books by school-story writers which are not part of a school-story series at all. Eva Löfgren's study of Dorita Fairlie Bruce's school stories necessarily neglected the Colmskirk novels, yet Bruce enthusiasts enjoy these late flowerings of her work, and it is a shame to leave them out simply because they do not fit within the genre for which she was chiefly known.[15]

People read story books primarily for the story. But fiction is also valuable as a historical source which informs us about the social context in which it was produced and the audience for whom it was originally intended. As Bridget Fowler observes in her study of romantic literature for women, *The Alienated Reader,* if archaeologists can reconstruct entire societies 'from the contents of prehistoric middens', then even the most formulaic fiction may reveal important clues about human societies, behaviour and needs.[16]

J. S. Bratton,[17] Judith Rowbotham[18] and Kimberley Reynolds[19] have demonstrated that girls' novels of the late nineteenth and early twentieth century often took up feminist ideas of the period which seemed to challenge conventional notions of femininity, yet nearly always came down on the side of tradition in the end. L. T. Meade, for example, one of the first school-story writers for girls, wrote of young women who went to university (*A Sweet Girl-Graduate,* 1891) and embarked on careers (*A Sister of the Red Cross,* 1901) but who, when faced with different lifestyle choices, took the familiar domestic path. Reynolds observes:

Indeed, one of the most interesting features of this new literature is the way it takes details from contemporary debate about the behaviour associated with the new imaging of women, and contrasts them with the internal values identified with old notions of femininity. The result is an essentially conservative attack on the 'girl of the period'.[20]

Rowbotham makes a similar point:

> Far from being immune to the pressures of social change, these novels display, in terms of an evolving body of tradition, the efforts of the conservative majority, especially in the middle classes, to reconcile the necessity for developments in the role of women with the accepted standards of feminine behaviour and aspirations.[21]

But she adds that 'this fiction mirrors the evolution of an acceptable role for middle-class women outside marriage and the nuclear family, with new invented "traditions" of its own'.[22] This latter tradition was developed by school-story writers in the twentieth century, many of them unmarried women, who often gave unusual prominence to unmarried career women in their novels.

The assumption that children's literature had an explicit role to play in inculcating appropriate gender expectations persisted well into the twentieth century and doubtless explains the uncritical welcome offered by parents, teachers and church officials to apparently sound novels by authors like Elsie Oxenham and Dorita Fairlie Bruce. But the period from the 1920s to the 1960s was very different from the late Victorian and Edwardian age, when the first wave of feminism was in full flood. By the 1920s that tide had begun to recede, and the 1930s and 1950s must be counted among the most reactionary decades ever for British women (the war years in between offering a brief relaxation of restraints). Turn-of-the-century literature for girls had to process and co-opt the radical models while reiterating the traditional message. Interwar and postwar fiction, on the other hand, had to appear to be conservative in order to be acceptable to the 'Reward' (school or Sunday school prize) market but, as long as authors toed the line outwardly and provided their heroines with suitably feminine occupations, heterosexual romance, marriage and motherhood, they had plenty of room to manoeuvre, and actually succeeded in pushing out the boundaries for their heroines.

By the 1950s, the 'separate spheres' philosophy which was an essential feature of the Victorian and early twentieth-century view of women's role had become deeply suspect; who could tell what women might get up to by themselves, unmonitored by men? In the second half of the century separate spheres was replaced by what Adrienne Rich was to call 'compulsory heterosexuality'; the enforced directing of women's energies towards men and away from women.[23] The more civil equality women achieved (in terms of access to legal rights, education, paid employment and other avenues to independence and power), the greater the ideological pressure to prioritise the interests of men and children, at the expense of other women – and themselves.

Kimberley Reynolds believes that images of women in girls' stories have changed very little since 1910:

> Girls in [mid-twentieth-century] stories may differ from those in stories written fifty years earlier in that they dress differently, are more active and experience more physical freedom, but their roles have remained more or less constant. ... Tomboys reform and turn into conventional, pretty, conformist and ministering young women. The domestic angel may have been replaced by a cricketer or sky nurse, but ultimately she seeks to please in much the same way as she always did.[24]

I agree that girls' stories of the early part of the twentieth century and those of the late twentieth century have much in common, but I am not so sure about the period in between. A glance at Anne Digby's contemporary Trebizon series is enough to demonstrate that within the familiar setting of the all-girls' boarding school a very different spirit prevails in the 1980s and 1990s from that which characterised the Jane Willard Foundation in the 1920s or the Chalet School through the 40 years of its history. As soon as she enters adolescence Digby's heroine Rebecca ceases to inhabit a world of women. Male teachers are a focus of attention and, while boys may not be physically present in the school, they are never far to away, and occupy a generous proportion of the girls' mental space which, in earlier school stories, would have been devoted to self-development and interests involving other girls. Only a late twentieth-century school story could have a title like *Boy Trouble at Trebizon* (1980).

Pamela Knights makes a similar point in her thoughtful comparison of Louisa May Alcott's novels for girls and Lois Lowry's *Anastasia* stories of 1979–91. Though the patriarchal influence pervades the nineteenth-century books, moulding the girls' behaviour even when the father is absent, 'Alcott's fiction, nevertheless, permits girls some autonomy'. In contrast,

Lowry's texts offer readers techniques for thinking about themselves and their options, and invite them to enjoy the seeming licence, whilst reassuring a parent that nothing has really changed: old-fashioned values are still in place.[25]

In this they resemble the feminist-influenced *fin-de-siècle* novels of 100 years ago.

But I think that the school stories of the early to mid-twentieth century are different. No one would call them feminist – a label which would certainly have horrified most of their authors – yet they resolutely refuse to play to a male gallery in the way that the novels of L. T. Meade and Anne Digby, in their different ways, do. In the pioneering late nineteenth and early twentieth centuries the roots of girls' school stories lay in the girls' schools themselves. These schools embodied a paradoxical mix of Victorian values and progressive, not to say feminist, ideals. Following in their wake, the girls' school story perpetuated the separate spheres ideology long after this had ceased to be fashionable in real life, providing a haven of woman-centredness in an increasingly male-conscious construction of femininity. How girls' school-story writers dealt with or, when they wanted to, ignored the heterosexual imperative in their depictions of growing up and grown-ups makes an interesting addition to the study of women's popular culture in the first half of the twentieth century.

The enduring popularity of so many of these books, however, suggests that these images and role models have a significance beyond the historical moment. Isabel Quigly was quite wrong when she wrote:

> Like every other form of fiction, girls' school stories have a sociological interest, telling us a great deal about their time and its attitudes; but it is hard to consider them as more than (occasionally charming) kitsch.[26]

For the thousands of girls and women who still read girls' school stories today, at the close of the twentieth century, and whose hackles must rise every time they read such a judgement, the stories must mean a great deal more than that.

Leaving aside the adult devotees, a large proportion of the 100,000-plus Chalet School books sold each year are read by children.[27] 'That is what makes our collections more than mere nostalgia,' remarks Martin Spence.

> [W]hen people...tell me patronisingly that the Chalet books are past their sell-by date, I simply say: 'Go into Smith's and look!' They never do, of course. They can't believe there ever was another world than this...[28]

In *A World of Girls* I argued that the appeal of school stories for successive generations of girls was the range of possibilities offered to them. That argument is further developed in *A World of Women*. My feeling is, indeed, that the portrayal of adult figures may be even more significant in this respect than that of girls, because adult role models offer child readers ideas about a future in which they might have some choice, something to strive for – we have much less choice about our childhood situation. Of course our 'choices' are necessarily limited and mediated by our circumstances; I might have loved to be like Oxenham's Joy Shirley when I grew up but, since I was neither beautiful nor rich, this dream could not realistically be sustained.

Though this did not put *me* off the books, I do not doubt that, for some readers, differences of privilege between school-story characters and themselves present a barrier to acceptance. There are few enough poor (or black or working-class) role models in these books, and a surfeit of wealthy white heroines. Certainly an Afro-American former fan of the Nancy Drew books, an immensely popular American series about a 'girl sleuth', declares that she 'can no longer read Nancy Drew as I did when I was younger and had no other frame of reference',[29] for the books, with their focus on one such wealthy white heroine, presented what seemed to her a denial of self. But other readers choose to read selectively, appreciating what speaks positively to them while weeding out the unpalatable bits – like the Chalet fan quoted by Helen McClelland in her biography of Elinor Brent-Dyer who had no sympathy with the religious preoccupation in the books, but found that 'somehow that rolled over me when young'.[30] And privileged lives have a positive fascination for many readers; as I observed in *A World of Girls*, boarding-school stories tend to attract those of us who never went to one.

Both *identity* (how we present ourselves to the world) and *subjectivity* (how we feel about ourselves) are made up of many different facets, of which race, sexuality, class and life experiences are all important, the proportions differing from individual to individual and from situation to situation. There are plenty of women who never think about their race, sexuality or class, but this is almost always because they are white, heterosexual and middle class, and thus enjoy the characteristics which are privileged in our society and which enable them to avoid the discrimination and stigmatising which routinely face black, lesbian and working-class women. But *gender* is an issue women can't ignore, because women are *not* the privileged gender in a patriarchal society. Whatever our circumstances, we cannot forget our common womanhood. For women fans, then, this is a point of contact with girls' school stories, even where other elements do not 'fit'.

And as this book demonstrates, these novels validate an extraordinary range of ways of being and acting as women. Whether you are married or unmarried, old or young, housewife or career woman, family-centred or woman-centred, or any combination of these, you can find characters positively presented in your position. If you don't much care for certain aspects of your real world or if you need an occasional breathing space, these books furnish an escape and a reinforcement of alternatives. If you are young enough to be moulded, or if there is room in your life to indulge a dream or make a change, these books could possibly point the way.

1 Young and Free

Like many girls, I did not want to grow up. Even at ten or eleven I realised that growing up, for girls, meant a curtailment of freedom. The shift from ankle socks to stockings, with their hideous accompaniment, the suspender belt, symbolised for me the psychological shift from tomboy to 'young lady'. Physical restrictions were parallelled by emotional ones. Why would anyone choose to be a woman? Men seemed to have all the freedom in the world.

Fortunately I was saved from any nascent transsexual drive by discovering, at just this stage in my life, Elsie Oxenham's Abbey books. It was not so much the school stories as the ones that dealt with heroines between school and marriage which most appealed to me – as they still do. To an eleven-year-old, the Joy and Jen of *The New Abbey Girls* and *The Abbey Girls Again* seemed to have everything a girl could want: they were *free*, having thrown off the constraints of school and not yet having acquired the shackles of marriage and motherhood; parental control was non-existent, and work no prerequisite for economic independence; and they were still *young* – no longer children, certainly, but not 'old' like Mrs Shirley or 'middle-aged' like Mary Devine. Reading these books, I realised that there was light at the end of the tunnel. I dreamed of the day when I, too, would be young and free. (Of course I never was, for, not being an heiress, when I was young I was not free, and when I became free – in the sense of having the kind of control over my life that the Abbey girls had – I was no longer young. But the dream sustained me.)

The Abbey books reconciled me to growing up. If I could

have that kind of independence as a woman, then a woman I would gladly be. During my teens, and indeed for decades afterwards, they fed a fantasy which could never be realised, but was so powerful for me that even today I cannot read *The Abbey Girls Again* without being eleven years old, admiring Joy and Jen as ever so grown up, seeing 30-year-old Mary as middle-aged. Elsie Oxenham was over 40 when she created these strong role models whose circumstances were in such contrast to mine – and hers. In practical terms they cannot be said to have influenced the course of my life (except that they brought me to live in Britain), but psychologically they had a tremendous impact. From that point on, my life was dedicated to the pursuit of independence, for myself and for other women, in a society predicated on the notion that a woman's rightful place was dependency within marriage. Elsie Oxenham would not have called herself a feminist, but she certainly helped to make me one.

On the surface, none of these books advocated a radical stance. Absolutely unquestioned, for example, was the idea that marriage was every girl's preferred destiny. Indeed, 'preferred' is too weak a word to describe the cultural insistence on marriage as the only truly acceptable outcome for our heroines, even though, of course, many women did not marry in these decades, including our three authors. The complementary notion, that 'ladies' should not engage in paid work, had less force after the First World War than before it, and even less after the Second, but it still exerted a strong influence on these writers, whose working heroines were always in a minority, their employment usually justified by reference to some family misfortune. A large part of the 'freedom' enjoyed by these early heroines, then, consisted in the fact that they were neither at school, nor at work, nor restricted by marriage and motherhood. If they *did* work, as increasingly school-story heroines went on to do, it was always at interesting, fulfilling careers of their own choice, not in the sort of humdrum, exploitative occupation with which, in truth, most real women had to be content.

By prolonging the period before their heroines married, as Oxenham did in many of her 1930s books, and by diminishing the effect of marriage on their lives when they finally wed, as did all three authors, the illusion of female independence was preserved. All this appealed to the young reader, whatever her generation. These heroines enjoyed the status of the young (the twentieth century has never accorded older women much respect or dignity), together with the maturity of the adult: an enviable combination, transient in life, but fixed in the pages of our favourite reading.

In real life, few young Englishwomen of the first half of this century had much freedom or independence in the modern sense. The women of Oxenham's and Bruce's first generation of heroines would not even have been able to vote until 1928, when the franchise was extended to women of 21 and over. Though single women had more property rights in law than married women, they would still have needed male guarantors for any moderately expensive contractual transaction. Property was almost always put in a man's name; mortgages were nearly impossible for women to get, whether married or single; and most women had too little income of their own, earned or unearned, to contemplate living away from home. Equal pay was decades away. Despite the popular image of the Bright Young Things, sexual morality was strict in the middle classes: abortion was illegal and contraception available only to the married – and even then it was frowned upon in many quarters, as Marie Stopes found.[1] Not surprisingly, most women who grew up in the interwar years have depicted themselves as being much 'younger', mentally, and less sophisticated than girls of the 1960s and later decades, especially in relation to the opposite sex. In many other respects, however, the interwar heroines seem older and more mature than my own and subsequent generations. This was because their creators were careful to use a variety of plot devices to remove them from the more extreme forms of patriarchal control – indeed, in some cases, apparently to remove them altogether from its orbit. One cannot help but speculate that, in the case of Oxenham and Brent-Dyer at least, this was done in a spirit of wish fulfilment. Both these women lived with their families until well into middle age, and neither ever enjoyed the financial means to be anything like as independent as her heroines.

Of our three authors, it was Oxenham who devoted most attention to heroines between school and marriage, but they were also important, in different ways, to Dorita Fairlie Bruce and Elinor M. Brent-Dyer. When Bruce took her heroines past their schooldays, she almost always used the traditional model of the romance or love story. Most of her school series are rounded off by one story about a heroine, grown up, who enjoys a brief period of freedom before finding her man. In *Dimsie Grows Up* (1924), Dimsie sets up her herbalism business, but decides to marry Peter; the business will continue, however, with the couple working together as joint medical and complementary practitioners. In *Toby at Tibbs Cross* (1943), Toby takes up farming, but succumbs to her childhood boyfriend Dick; in *Nancy Calls the Tune* (1944), Nancy becomes a church organist and marries the minister. Three of the four Colmskirk books end with an engagement; only *Triffeny* (1950) is solely concerned with a young woman's path to maturity, without any love interest. The Colmskirk books are not school stories, but they closely resemble Oxenham's Abbey romances of the interwar years, only they are set in the 1940s and 1950s when school stories were in eclipse. Each is concerned with a separate but interconnected cast of characters, among whom one, Julia Lendrum, functions as a constant linking thread. Julia, like Triffeny, grows up but does not marry: she, too, is young and free.

For Elinor Brent-Dyer, the sheer length and breadth of the Chalet series mean that all ages and life circumstances are encompassed. But unlike Bruce and Oxenham, Brent-Dyer rarely makes a feature of romance; it is simply one stage in her heroines' development, part of the ongoing story. *The Chalet School in Exile* (1938) takes Jo Bettany from youthful independence through romance, engagement, marriage and motherhood in the course of a single book whose primary focus is something else altogether: the Chalet School's removal from Nazi-occupied Austria to wartime Guernsey. Even the recently discovered *Jean of Storms* (1930), which purports to be a conventional love story, is much more concerned with Jean's coming to maturity through assuming the guardianship of two little girls. The romance itself is, arguably, the least successful aspect of the book.

Elsie Oxenham took romance more seriously, especially in her later books where every story seems to end with an engagement. But her greatest fascination was clearly with women's emotional growth to maturity and, because most of her series have several heroines, she is able to offer a wide range of variations on the theme. Each of the Abbey girls, for instance, has her turn. Readers may follow Joan (briefly in *The Abbey Girls Go Back to School*, 1922), Joy and then Jen (at greater length through the novels of the 1920s) as they negotiate the process of growing up; then, in the following decade, she starts the process all over again with the second-generation heroines, Rosamund and Maidlin. Unlike Bruce and Brent-Dyer, Oxenham – always a leisurely writer – often took several books to describe the process. Though described as 'romances', many of these volumes are without romance in the sense of a heterosexual love interest, men being tangential or wholly absent from the plot.

Clearly, these are not romances as understood by Ethel M. Dell or Daphne du Maurier, contemporary exponents of the genre.[2] Lynette Muir suggests that Oxenham used the word 'romance' in an archaic sense:

The construction of the series is exactly similar to the medieval romance cycle. A number of permanent characters alternate with individual girls who appear for one book then vanish again, their story complete. They are drawn to the Abbey and the Hamlet Club as knights in the old romances are drawn to the Court of King Arthur and the Fellowship of the Round Table.[3]

Equally plausibly, the novels can be viewed as extended love stories, in which not only do most of the central characters, after many vicissitudes, get their man, but the author's own strong feelings for her heroines shine through.

Like Dorita Fairlie Bruce, Oxenham turned to the more conventional form of romance in the 1940s. *Pernel Wins* (1942) and *Daring Doranne* (1945), for example, are plainly love stories, though in making the heroines heiresses Oxenham manages to remove any sense that, in marrying the men they love, they are capitulating to patriarchal control. By then the particular form of the 'young and free' stage in a girl's life Oxenham had so eloquently described in the interwar years was virtually obsolete; girls now went to college or got a job; they did not sit around wondering what to do with their lives. Curiously reluctant to give her heroines professional careers (though they might dance or sing), Oxenham found herself having to shorten the interval between school and marriage until, like Nanta and Littlejan in the Abbey books of the 1950s, they were marrying at nineteen and becoming mothers exactly nine months later.

For a young woman of the school-story generations to enjoy 'freedom' in the years before her marriage, four conditions were necessary: economic independence, freedom from parental control, emotional maturity and space. However elusive in real life, these conditions were more often than not present in the growing-up novels of the school-story writers, who could – and did – manoeuvre the text to ensure that their heroines achieved their goals.

Economic independence

In interwar Britain it was customary for young, middle-class women to live at home with their parents. If they came from monied families, they were often discouraged from taking paid employment. 'Father is rather bigoted about girls earning their living when they don't actually require to,' Dorita Fairlie Bruce's Nancy confides in a book of 1935.[4] If less well-off, they would have to get a job and this might entail living in lodgings or a hostel. Women's wages being less than men's, few could afford to rent their own flat, let alone buy one. In every case, dependence was assumed – on parents or relatives and, later, it would be confidently predicted, on a husband. The whole rationale behind paying women less than men was that the latter would have families to support while the former would be supported by their families.

In order to be free, therefore, a measure of financial independence was essential. Elsie Oxenham solved that difficulty by making most of her heroines rich. Several are heiresses (Eilidh, Joy, Maidlin, Doranne) and most of the rest are not merely comfortable, but wealthy beyond her readers' wildest dreams. There are characters in Oxenham's books who have to work for a living, who come from modest or (more usually) 'reduced' circumstances, like Mary and Biddy Devine and the Bellanne sisters. But they get to benefit from being drawn into the circles of the wealthy: Mary can give up her boring office job to come to the Abbey as Joy's 'secretary'; Anne Bellanne becomes Maidlin's housekeeper. Oxenham's enthusiasm for raising ordinary middle-class girls to great wealth therefore functions as a device which not only frees them from dependence (Joy Shirley had started off dependent on her grandfather's charity) but helps other women too, like Mary, who is now 'freed' to write her books. (As we shall see in Chapter 3, Mary is free only up to a point; like the archetypal maiden aunt, she is expected to drop everything and rush to the help of Joy or Jen in any family crisis.)

Dorita Fairlie Bruce demonstrates that a fortune is not a prerequisite for freedom: a small inheritance will do. In *The Serendipity Shop* (1947), Merran Lendrum uses her legacy – an antique shop on the western coast of Scotland – as an opportunity to move herself and her young sister away from the relatives in London they have been living with. Contrary to expectation she does not sell the shop and invest the capital so realised; she chooses to run it as a business to support the two of them, while they live over the shop. Though she has lost her genteel idleness, she has gained control over her life; her money is now her own, to use as she wishes.

The *removal* of wealth may have the same effect. Oxenham's Rosamund, living off an allowance from her father, suddenly finds herself without means when he remarries and withdraws his support. Of course Ros need not fear destitution; she has lived for years with Joy, Lady Marchwood, and Joy has enough money to maintain a dozen penniless girls. But Rosamund's pride will not allow her to contemplate dependence and she leaves the Abbey to go and help some relatives run a tea-room and craft shop in Sussex.[5] Brent-Dyer's Madge Bettany, too, is inspired to set up her school on the death of her guardian and the loss of all financial support.[6]

It may be objected that, because they have to work, these heroines are not really free in the sense that Joy and Jen were. This is true, but they are still their own mistresses: girls' story heroines are resolutely self-employed; they do not work for others. Madge starts a school, Merran manages her shop, Mollie Thurston (in Brent-Dyer's *They Both Liked Dogs*, 1938) is a concert pianist; several heroines write. Merran assures her aunt, who fears a loss of status for the girls, that 'everybody [works] nowadays, and quite a lot of people keep shops'.[7] Later in the same novel, Merran's resistance to Sam Bartle's offer to buy her out (he wants to build a department store on the land) expresses itself in terms of freedom versus dependence:

> Then a picture rose swiftly before her of the quaint old square demolished, and in its place some glittering monstrosity of a model store flaunting its ostentation to the public gaze, with herself working in it as an employee of Bartle's, forced by her dependent position to conform to his whims and fancies, no longer free to follow her own ideas and inclinations in the work she loved. . . . 'I take a certain pride in owning this scrap of the town, and I prefer to be my own mistress.'[8]

Though money is plainly a prerequisite for freedom, it is not, on its own, enough. Indeed, as Oxenham shows, independent wealth could be a positive hindrance to our heroines of the 1920s and 1930s because of the maxim that ladies should not work. That Oxenham and Bruce accepted this already anachronistic notion is indicative of a Victorian world-view neither ever outgrew. Even Brent–Dyer, who was never personally in a position to live off anyone, allowed her heroine Jo Bettany to leave school in 1935 without a job. But this apparent compliance with conventional notions of middle-class femininity is undercut by our authors' obvious reluctance to allow their heroines to remain idle. These young women *want* to work, or at least do good works; but they do not want to be forced into some dull or unpleasant employment not of their own choosing, as so many women were, of course, in real life. Brent–Dyer's Jo feels directionless after she leaves school, until helping out with some teaching and getting down to her writing restore her confidence. Bruce sought excuses to enable her characters to get out and work in spite of their means. The advent of the Second World War was a godsend to her, since it meant Nancy (*Nancy Calls the Tune*) and Toby (*Toby at Tibbs Cross*) could engage in interesting and worthwhile employ-ment while the men who would have done the work were away defending their country.

These books reflect the very real social contradictions of their times. In the eyes of their Victorian-born creators, Jo, Nancy and Toby belonged to a class where paid work was 'unnecessary' (read: undesirable) for girls; their readers, however, increasingly came from circles where girls routinely took jobs after leaving school, and would certainly have expected to make a contribution to the country's war effort. No girl could read these books – not even Oxenham's – and not grasp that work was important, even for women. But no one could read them without realising the value of money, which enabled you to choose the type and conditions of that work. These heroines did not work for money; in a range of different ways, money worked for them.

Freedom from parental control

As well as financial independence, to be truly free girls needed to get away from their families. In 1928 Virginia Woolf named 'A room of one's own' as a prerequisite for feminine achieve-ment, but for energetic, idealistic escapees from convention like Vera Brittain and Winifred Holtby, a whole flat (with a maid) was needed. Both women did have paid work, but such luxury could be sustained only by an allowance from their parents' – something which was not available to the vast majority of young women. These, if they could not remain in the family home, were forced to live in lodgings or work-sponsored hostels, a style of accommodation which would not have been seen as suitable by old-fashioned parents. The Abbey girls' fascination with their communal living arrangements at folk-dancing vacation schools betrays their complete unfamiliarity with what they would have seen as 'roughing it'.[10]

The unmarried daughter at home, caring for ageing parents and at everybody's beck and call, was a Victorian cliché that took on a depressing reality for many, many women well into the twentieth century. In *The Abbey Girls Go Back to School* (1922), we learn that this is to be the fate of Jen Robins. At the age of sixteen she is removed by her parents from Miss Macey's school in Wycombe to go home to Yorkshire. 'Heaps of money, you know, and a big country house, and Jen's the only girl,' Joan tells Cicely.

> '...All they want is to get her through school as soon as possible and have her home to help her mother and be company for her. If she knows a little, and can play and sing a little, and speak French a little, and dance... that's all they want. Jen's pretty and smart, and has done well as far as she's gone; she isn't shy and has good manners... So she's... to go home and be an ornament to society, I suppose. I should think she'd die in a month!'[11]

Jen, of course, does not die; she makes the most of her lonely exile, getting involved in village activities and starting dancing classes for the local children. But when opportunities arise for her to come south to see her friends, she seizes them. First there is the month at summer school in Cheltenham. Then her father's illness necessitates treatment in London, so parents and daughter take a flat in 'Town', as Oxenham always calls it, allowing her to see plenty of Joy close at hand in Oxfordshire and her old school chum Jack (Jacqueline) who lives with her parents in Harley Street.

Often the girls who have to go home are the most able ones, the ones who were leaders at school and would have welcomed further education and a career. One such was Bruce's Sheila Macnab, Captain of Springdale: 'Her sister got married all of a heap, and her mother wanted her at home. Sheila's the sort of person who would be wanted; she's good at stepping into gaps.'[12] Their horizons shrinking, their daily routines dictated by others, such women often ended up with no life of their own. The role survived well into the 1950s. In Oxenham's *Rachel in the Abbey* (1951), Littlejan is summarily withdrawn from school to help her mother 'in a crisis'. All that has happened is that Janice is having another baby and her nurse/companion is temporarily unavailable. No one in the book disputes the decision, not even Littlejan herself. And although readers recognise a plot device when they see one – Littlejan must withdraw from the Abbey to allow her dependent friends to move centre-stage – we balk at it when it means the disappearance of a popular character whom we meet again only years later, already married (perhaps in a desperate effort to have her own life).[13] In Brent-Dyer's *Bride Leads the Chalet School* (1953), Mrs Bettany has a major operation and Peggy, her eldest daughter, former Head Girl of the Chalet School and currently enjoying a year abroad at its finishing school in Switzerland, faces the prospect of giving up school to keep house for her. 'It was certain that Mrs Bettany would not be able to see to the housekeeping for many a long day to come and who so suitable to take her place as her eldest daughter?'[14] At least the mother's illness provides some excuse in this case, but there is no question of Peggy's twin brother having to leave school. In the event, a widowed aunt steps in and Peggy's education is saved.

Clearly, no novel about a daughter-at-home was going to be very popular with young readers, though plenty were written in the nineteenth century, evidently in an effort to reconcile women to their situation.[15] The challenge for our authors was how to extricate heroines who would naturally have assumed this role. And the answer, more easily available to the writer of fiction than in real life, was to kill off the parents.

It is a truism that fiction for children contains a disproportionate number of absent or dead parents: how else could an author endow the child heroes with the necessary independence of action? But with novels for girls, written by women, this factor takes on an added significance. It was certainly a favoured device of Oxenham, Bruce and Brent-Dyer, all three of them unmarried daughters. Madge and Jo Bettany start the Chalet series already orphaned. Oxenham gives Joy Shirley neither father nor mother, only an aunt who very quickly declines into premature senility and death in her fifties. Jen loses both her parents during her 'young and free' years; to do her justice, Oxenham introduces these deaths into the storyline at the time when her own dearly loved parents died, which makes their portrayal particularly poignant, but she was in her forties at the time and Jen isn't yet twenty. Rosamund's parents are absent from the moment she enters the series; her mother dies at a sanatorium in Switzerland, her father remarries and promptly dies, and she too is left an orphan when scarcely out of her teens. Maidlin is parentless from childhood. The same is true of several less important characters: the Devines, the Bellannes, Maid's cousins Rachel and Damaris. Bruce's Dimsie is not an orphan, but her mother is absent at the beginning of her school career and gently ineffectual thereafter; her father dies a year after she leaves school, and her mother, too, is gone by the last book in the series. Toby is motherless. Merran and Julia are orphaned. Very few characters in the books of these three authors have two normal, active parents.

Readers familiar with the conventions of children's literature tend to take the absence or removal of parents for granted. Psychologists have pointed out that children's reading allows them to explore unfamiliar, even dangerous ideas and experiences in their imagination, from the safety of the printed page, preparing them to meet similar challenges, perhaps, when grown up. Without the parental control of real life, a child can imagine herself powerful, able to deal with things she would be terrified to encounter in reality.[16]

But there is a contradiction in these growing-up novels for girls, in which the danger element is not usually central. They are more often concerned with emotional growth within a community of women, where not only might one expect a mother to occupy a central place, mentoring girls in the caring role, but the girls themselves are being prepared for motherhood. Boys of the time were not encouraged to see their future role primarily in terms of fatherhood, but motherhood was a major *raison d'être* for the female sex. To write the mother out of the story or, worse, to allow her to decline into helpless dependence in middle age smacks of misogyny, not to speak of ageism; these are gestures which many readers feel uncomfortable with, even as children, and particularly when they reach middle age themselves.

Society is, of course, both misogynistic and ageist and we cannot be too surprised when authors internalise and collude in their own oppression. But it seems clear that, in the 1920s and 1930s, removing parental control was genuinely perceived as a prerequisite to endowing the young women of these novels with the sort of agency their authors and readers would love to have had. All three authors were consciously or unconsciously pointing out the distinction between the relatively powerless wife and mother of their Victorian childhoods and the 'modern', independent young woman of their readers' generation. Of course, many Victorian wives and mothers did not see themselves as powerless, though it is worth bearing in mind how restricted they were in law (married women were not even guardians of their own children, for example) and in custom: even those with a good education could not, in society's eyes, make use of it in paid employment after marriage. The economic power of husbands ensured men's unchallenged domination in the family.

The 1920s enhanced women's legal and social situation in many areas. Legislation conferred the vote and improved property, divorce and custody rights, while women's work in the First World War ensured that they could never again be patronised in quite the same way. But the forces of convention were strong, and the 1920s also saw a reaction against women's increased independence. Women were forced back to the home, jobs were reserved for men, and marriage assumed still greater importance in women's lives. Fuelled by the economic depression, this anti-feminist drive grew stronger in the 1930s. In the face of this ideological pressure, our authors had to struggle to maintain the sense of independence for their heroines; and one acceptable way to do it in a novel was to kill off the restraining parental influence. Men were largely absent from these books, an acurate reflection of the distant authoritarian models of the time; but mothers might have been there, urging femininity, holding their daughters back. Our authors symbolically destroyed the old image of the outwardly powerless, but domestically restricting, mother, replacing it with the much more attractive, unrealistically powerful daughter.

Where parents do exist in these interwar novels, they are certainly seen as inhibiting factors. Jen's chum Jack is not permitted, at eighteen, to go alone to dance parties, even those taking place just around the corner. If her parents are out of town, and there is no one to collect her, she can't go.[17] Jen's mother makes her promise that the chauffeur will accompany her when she calls at Mary's flat one evening, although only Mary and her sister live there.[18] As Joy moves towards middle age in the Abbey books of the 1930s, she too starts to act more and more like a brake on her 'adopted' daughters:

'Can you imagine Maidie in business? The very idea is ridiculous. – Did you think of being a shorthand-typist, Maid? Or a children's nurse, or a cook? Or perhaps you think you could teach something?... It's a crazy idea, and Maid will have to admit it. She isn't fitted for that sort of life, and it's quite unnecessary. – Now, Maidie, don't keep on talking about it. It's impossible. I'd never agree.'[19]

After the Second World War attitudes changed. Middle-class parents became less distant from their children, partly because there were fewer (or no) servants to mediate the relationship, and partly because suburban life, with its limited local recreation, encouraged families to spend time together at home. While these material changes were hardly evident in the Chalet or Abbey books, their authors still partook of the ideological shift: the old authoritarianism declined, and happy families became the social ideal. This shift was strongly reflected in children's literature in the 1950s and 1960s, and partly accounts for the decline in the school story and its replacement with the family-style adventure tale. Mothers are much more present in the postwar series stories, and Joan in the Abbey books and Jo in the Chalet books are both portrayed as modern mothers.

There was another reason for keeping mothers on the scene in the later series books, of course. For these mothers were the series' original heroines – Joy, Dimsie, Jo – and it would hardly do to kill them off simply to grant their daughters independence! Instead, our authors tended to exaggerate and idealise the mother–daughter bond, partly in keeping with the ideology of the time, but partly in order to keep control in the hands of the characters their creators loved most. Jo dominates the Chalet series into her forties. The second generation of Abbey girls never really breaks free – never really grows up.

Emotional maturity

A further component of freedom is emotional maturity. Once again, Oxenham's procession of Abbey girls goes through the process of achieving this in ever more complex ways. Frankly, this is what these relatively plotless books are about. It would be easy to see this emotional growth in crudely psychoanalytic terms: young women making the adjustment from the world of girls, in which their emotional energies are focused on other young women, to the world of heterosexual romance and marriage, in which their emotional energies are refocused on men (or a man) and then children. Certainly the growing-up model in many of these books is of an 'awakening' to heterosexual love. But two factors force us to modify this equation. One is that the process of achieving emotional maturity often incorporates, or is wholly concerned with, issues other than falling in love: breaking away from the family circle, for example (Rosamund); coming to terms with the death of parents (Jen); facing difficult challenges or choices (Maidlin); forging a career (Jo, Dimsie, Triffeny). The other is that, however much our heroines may appear to prioritise their husbands and children, they actually continue to inhabit a world of women.

We see little of the emotional growth of Oxenham's Joan, the 'good' Abbey girl. In one novel, at a folk-dancing summer school, she meets a man. By the start of the next book in the series, she is married to him.[20] Though *The Abbey Girls Go Back to School* is a popular book, I think that Oxenham's lack of concern for Joan's emotional development detracts from the plot's plausibility. Joan, hitherto an interesting character who engaged the reader's sympathy, vanishes into boring domesticity and remains a colourless cipher for the rest of the series. Oxenham does nothing to dispel young readers' fears that this is what marriage does to women. When Jen invites Joan and Cicely to an evening engagement with the female crowd, for instance,

'I'll have to ask Jack,' Joan said doubtfully. 'I'd love it, of course. If he can come, or if he has anything else to do and doesn't need me, I'll come like a shot.'

'Must be a fag always having to consult a man,' Joy remarked ... 'You'll not find me ever taking a man in tow!'[21]

Perhaps conscious of the loss to Joan's characterisation, in her retrospective Abbey titles Oxenham returns to Joan's 'young and free' days, offering a much more rounded picture.[22]

In 1922, however, it seems that Oxenham felt that Joan, as well as her mother, was too restraining an influence on her 'bad' Abbey girl, Joy. She thereupon removed them both from centre-stage, somehow managing to link marriage and premature senility in one young reader's mind, and allowing Joy, until now a much less attractive character, to move into the limelight.

Joy is without doubt Oxenham's greatest creation. Some fans prefer other characters, but the way Oxenham shifts our vision of Joy from the selfish, fun-loving tomboy of the first three Abbey tales to the earnest, self-doubting adult of *The New Abbey Girls* (1923) and *The Abbey Girls Again* (1924) is a literary *tour de force*. In *The Abbey Girls in Town* (1925), we are treated to a view of Joy as Mary sees her – glamorous and bountiful – and also as Ruth sees her: fascinating, but self-absorbed, 'kind, gracious, friendly, a benefactress trying to help all who needed her,' but not 'an understanding friend who could enter into another's feelings'.[23] Yet with all her imperfections, Joy still attracts and deserves love. In the later books in the series she becomes less sympathetic, more one-dimensional, but then all the characters do.

Joy's constant struggle is with her thoughtlessness and selfishness. She has to learn to think of others besides herself. Jen's near death in a motorcycle accident, for which Joy is to blame; the arrival of fourteen-year-old Maidlin, whom Joy has been asked to bring up; her desire to use her wealth for the benefit of others; and her exposure to real social work in the East End of London, all combine to produce a new, more mature Joy. She decides that she will thenceforth 'do something worth while, and make people feel it was worth having me round, instead of being no use to any one and just pleasing myself and having a good time'.[24] Motherhood finally transforms her but she never entirely loses her self-centredness: that is part of her charm, and the effectiveness of her portrayal.

Jen's development is more conventional. Jen, like Jo Bettany of the Chalet books, resists growing up. Then, like Jo, and also like Bruce's Dimsie, she meets her man but does not immediately recognise that he is her mate. For Jen the turning point comes when she realises her father is dying, and turns to Kenneth for support.

But Jen is more interesting than this synopsis would suggest. Though three years younger than Joy, she is already (and she remains) the more mature, thoughtful and balanced of the two. It is Jen who helps Rosamund through a difficult patch in her relationship with Maidlin, when Ros is fired up by new experiences away from the Abbey and Maidlin seems stuck in the home routine. Jen advises Rosamund never to refuse help to anyone who asks for it, even if the request seems babyish. 'Would you go on helping people for ever?' Rosamund asks curiously; and Jen replies:

> 'As long as they seemed to need it. I'd trust them to grow up some day; but I wouldn't force them. Some people grow very slowly. Mary always says one part of her didn't even begin to grow till after she was thirty.'[25]

Rosamund's route is a harder one. She has always had bigger ambitions than Jen, who claims to want no more than a big house full of children (which she gets). Rosamund is a born manager, but it is out of the question for her to pursue a career; and she is not content with anonymous do-gooding, teaching classes in the village, lending a hand in Joy's home. She wants to make her name. After her father remarries, she explains to Joy and Jen:

> 'I was marking time, till Father needed me. Now he'll never need me. It's not exactly a question of money and earning my living. . . . But it is a question of doing something to earn my right to be alive. . . . If I were Mary and could write

books, I'd be satisfied. Or if I had Maid's voice, I wouldn't ask anything better than to use it. If I had a home and children, as you two have, I'd feel I was filling my place and being worth while. But having none of these things, and no particular gifts, I have to look round and find my work. It may be conceit, and if it is I'm sorry; but I do want to be Somebody, Somebody who matters!'[26]

Joy at first ridicules Rosamund's yearning for a shop where she could have 'piles of boxes, all sizes, and pack things in each'. She tries to hang on to her older adopted daughter: 'Can't you put our feelings before your own? Why should your sudden craving for adventure upset all our lives?'[27] But in the end Rosamund's determination wins out and Joy lets her go.

We follow her modest entry into business, helping out in her aunts' tea-room, setting up her own craft shop. She goes to cookery classes, emerging with a first-class diploma, and learns to weave on her own loom. By the time she has taken on her pathetic stepmother and forced her to give up her baby for adoption (by Rosamund herself), we recognise that Ros's gifts need a wider canvas for their proper exercise. What she craves is not exactly a career but, frankly, power; she knows she is a leader and a good manager, but how can an upper-middle-class girl have any real impact on the world? Oxenham obligingly contrives for the baby half-brother to give her access to titled relatives of whom we have never previously heard, thence to the disabled son of an earl, thence by design disguised as accident to a fitting role as Countess of Kentisbury with a castle of her own.[28] By spreading this fairy-tale across half a dozen books, Oxenham almost manages to convince us that this was the job Ros was waiting for all along. 'Next week I have to take up the burden of that old family title and try to do my bit for Kentisbury.'[29] Sheila Ray and Stella Waring describe Rosamund as the epitome of the great American dream, 'the heroine who achieves through her own ability'.[30]

Brought up in the shadow of bossy Rosamund, Maidlin needs to be entrusted with responsibility, to show that she can cope alone after Rosamund has gone. 'Joy, you've been more than good to her; but you've been too good,' Ruth points out. 'She hasn't had a chance to grow up. And then you all call her "Kid" and "Babe"! No wonder it gets on her nerves.'[31] In *Biddy's Secret* (1932), Maidlin gets her chance to break away. Responding to an appeal for help from an old friend, Maidlin flees to France without telling anyone, rescues Biddy (and her baby, the 'secret' of the title), and returns to Joy's reluctant acceptance of her maturity. *Biddy's Secret* could have been called *Maidlin Grows Up*, for that is really what it is about. But Maid remains a slow developer: a dozen more Abbey books must pass before she gains full emotional independence. As Ruth once observed, 'You live so much inside yourself that I believe your growing up will have to be done there.'[32] Maidlin does not marry until she is in her late twenties (in *Maid of the Abbey*, 1943), and, when she does, she chooses a man who will not only allow her to combine family life with a career on the concert platform, but will positively facilitate it.

If Oxenham's books provide the most extensive interrogation, Dorita Fairlie Bruce and Elinor Brent-Dyer also deal with emotional growth in their novels. Bruce is limited because she chose to give herself only one volume (except in Dimsie's case) in which to bring her heroines to maturity; she is also rather more interested in plot than Oxenham, giving correspondingly less attention to character development. But her Triffeny (in the novel of that name, 1950) must evolve from a thoughtless, self-centred schoolgirl who, expecting to be sent to art school, finds herself working for her aunt instead. In the two years spanned by the novel, Triffeny comes to identify herself completely with the family business, and takes over as manager (at seventeen) from her aunt on the latter's conveniently early death.

Brent-Dyer's Jo takes longer to make the transition. Her

youthful reluctance to grow up is signalled as early as the fifth book in the Chalet series:

> 'Just look at Gisela! Three years ago, she was our head girl – and a jolly good one, too. Now, she's married, and has settled down to keeping house and darning Gottfried's socks. Then Wanda goes and marries Friedel, and has a flat to run. Bernhilda is betrothed, and will be married in December, and even if Kurt *is* your brother, Marie, and quite decent – I must say I think they needn't all be in such a hurry to grow up.'[33]

Her friends laugh at her: 'Jo would like to stay a babe for ever!' In *The Chalet Girls in Camp* (1932), she warns the man who, unknown to any of us, she will one day marry: 'I'll be like Jo March in *Little Women* and "wear my hair in two tails till I'm twenty!"'[34] Still resisting in her last term at school, she is firmly taken in hand by her friends. Frieda draws her attention to the many old girls of the school, now happily settled in their own homes. But Jo objects hastily: 'I certainly don't want any husbands. And we've heaps of babies at Die Rosen as it is. . .'[35] By the end of the term, however, she seems able to accept Marie's engagement with more or less equanimity, causing her sister to reflect:

> Joey is beginning to grow up, and to grow up happily. This past year has done much for her. The child has given way to the girl; and the girl will be lost in the woman, and Joey will be happy and contented.[36]

The suggestion is that the transformation is due to Jo's having successfully discharged the duties of Head Girl over that year, forcing her to become mature in using her undoubted powers of influence for the benefit of others.

Jo's anxiety at the prospect of long domestic days stretching out when she leaves school ('It does *not* appeal to me after the full life we lead here – it seems so – so *little*, somehow')[37] is fortunately allayed when she is called back almost immediately to help out teaching at the Chalet School. The headmistress suggests: 'If you are going to write school-stories, you ought to have some idea of school-life from *our* point of view.'[38] Jo profits from this exercise, proves herself an able teacher, and writes her first book, which is accepted for publication.

Two terms later, Jo clearly thinks like an adult. 'D'you know, Bill,' she remarks to Miss Wilson as they sit the night out stranded with a party of girls in a charabanc on a flooded road outside Salzburg, 'it's a queer thing, but since I've left school, you people seem to be getting years nearer my own age.'[39] This gentle progression towards adulthood means that the romance, marriage and motherhood that arrive for Jo in *The Chalet School in Exile* (1940) are not improbable. It is known that Brent-Dyer wrote a novel called *Two Chalet Girls in India* which was never published, and is now missing: this might conceivably have been Brent-Dyer's 'Jo Grows Up' novel. As it is, much of Jo's growing up occurs gradually between books without any of the forced breaking away to maturity that Elsie Oxenham's characters have to undergo.

Space

In an era when most young women went from family home to marital home, the idea of setting up with friends in a flat or hostel would have seemed quite exciting. Oxenham, who lived with her parents till well into middle age, and then with a sister in a very small house, makes the most of this, in her descriptions of Rosamund's cottage, for which all the Abbey folk provide housewarming presents, or of the Pixie's London flat, which seemed to one young Australian reader the most romantic prospect in the world.[40] Brent-Dyer, too, lived with her mother and stepfather; after the latter's death, the two women shared what was admittedly a large house first with an entire school (for ten years) and then with a succession of lodgers. Their experience was probably more typical for women of their generation than that of Dorita Fairlie Bruce, who, alone of our three authors, enjoyed a home of her own. But she clearly revelled in it, her enthusiasm coming through in the descriptions of her Colmskirk heroines, Merran and Prim, as they furnish their apartments.[41] Physical independence is clearly important for young women who want to be free: space to spread out in, and control over their environment − two factors much restricted in the family home or lodgings.

Authors recognised, however, that a home of one's own was inconceivable for most young women; it was too expensive, too daring, too scary − and 'unnecessary', if a perfectly adequate room was available in the home of a parent or relative. There is no question of Bruce's Dimsie or Brent-Dyer's Jo moving away, for example. For the woman who had to earn her own living, a compromise was the hostel, which met the limited purses of most working 'girls' and the objections of those who decried female independence. Hostels for working women appeared towards the end of the nineteenth century to provide a 'home away from home' for the burgeoning female workforce in the cities. Mollie Hughes described in her autobiography how she lived with her friend Annie Rogers in a 'Ladies' Residential Chambers', where they could be 'free of landladies for ever, and be able to eat our rice-pudding under our own fig-tree'.[42] This captures the sense of freedom exactly.

By the 1920s such hostels were not always such grand or desirable places; certainly women were sometimes subject to what we would now regard as highly restrictive controls on their personal freedom. These are not evident, however, in Oxenham's evocation of hostel life in her descriptions of St

Mary's in the Swiss Oberland (where Ven and her friends stay) and Rainbow Corner in London (where Daphne, Elsa, Pernel and Doranne have their flats).

> 'It's really a girls' hotel. ... It's divided into little suites of two, three, or four rooms, and a bathroom and kitchen to each, so that you can do your own cooking, if you like. There's a big restaurant on the ground floor... Downstairs, there's a lounge, and a reading-room, where you have to be quiet so that people can study, and a hall with a piano, and quite a jolly garden.'[43]

Housing whole communities of women, these hostels had the advantage of providing companionship and security – and meals – but also allowing individuals to express themselves in the choice of furniture and decor. The relish of Oxenham's descriptions of hostels (later she moved on to whole towns, like Rainbows – see *Margery Meets the Roses*, 1947) catches the excitement with which young women must have greeted these opportunities for semi-independent living:

> The door opened into a cheerful room with yellow-washed walls, cream matting on the dark-stained floor, dark wooden doors to the built-in wardrobe and cupboards, and a big window. It was furnished with one big table and one small one; two plain rush-seated chairs and one big wicker one; a small electric stove for heating; and in an alcove, a little bed and toilet articles. ... 'Isn't it the jolliest little place?... And when I've furnished it, it will be simply beautiful. ... Perhaps green curtains?'[44]

There is no suggestion of dragon-like matrons, doors locked at eleven or prohibitions on male visitors in any of these stories. Perhaps Oxenham was unaware that these existed in real life. Her young women appear to have all the freedom they want, though this does not seem to include bringing men back to their rooms.

Claiming men's territory

The idea of space encompasses not only the physical space of room or home, but also the symbolic space of men's territory, which school-story heroines calmly and confidently invade. Heroines like Rosamund Kane, for example, take on leadership roles; Joy's wealth gives her enormous power and influence; the Chalet girls appropriate masculine language (for Tom Gay – a girl despite her name – prefect Daisy Venables is 'a gentleman') and masculine goals such as the profession of medicine. But perhaps one of the most noticeable ways in which Oxenham and Brent-Dyer claim men's territory for their heroines is by placing them in the magical setting of the Swiss Oberland.

Exotic settings have been a feature of children's novels throughout the twentieth century. It is perhaps not surprising, therefore, given the British middle class's love affair with the Alps in the preceding century, that Switzerland provided the backdrop for so many girls' school stories. In fact Elsie Oxenham was the first author to locate an English school in the Alps (in *The Two Form-Captains*, 1921), with Elinor Brent-Dyer's Chalet School series, originating in the Austrian Tyrol, following in 1925. Both women had visited the Alps as tourists, Oxenham on a number of occasions before and after the First World War, Brent-Dyer in the early 1920s.

We are so accustomed now to the idea of Swiss finishing schools for girls that it is hard to credit that, before the First World War, the Alps were largely male territory. The Alpine Club, formed in 1857, excluded women. 'From the very beginning, therefore, climbing – certainly of the organised, establishment variety – was a male-oriented preserve,' explain

Bill Birkett and Bill Peascod.[45] There were, of course, a tiny number of women mountaineers whose exploits – like Lucy Walker's ascent of the Matterhorn in 1871, only six years after the ill-fated British expedition which claimed four lives – shocked and astonished their contemporaries. One of the climbing Pigeon sisters remarked that 'many members of the Alpine Club would not speak to us'.[46] Women might accompany husbands, fathers or brothers on Alpine holidays[47] or, like 'Miss Jemima', join Thomas Cook's escorted tours of Switzerland from 1863 onwards.[48] But when Arnold Lunn traced the connections between the Swiss Alps and the English Romantic movement, his use of the masculine noun was not misjudged: 'Men lifted up their eyes to the hills to rediscover the spiritual values which were clouded by the smoke and the grime of the industrial revolution.'[49] Women, meanwhile, stayed at home, excluded from this transcendental challenge.

Lunn quoted a German contemporary who drew a contrast between the Englishman's relationship to the Alps and that of his own compatriots:

> The Englishmen were ... financially independent and in a position to develop their personalities by free choice of a career. The German, on the other hand, came from a narrow circle and was forced to devote himself throughout life to a restricted calling. . . . To the young German then, as now, the mountains appealed primarily as an avenue of escape from restrictions. Among the mountains he sought to develop his own personality. . . .[50]

Substitute 'woman' for 'German' and you get a sense of what the Alps meant to the few Englishwomen who had the good fortune to travel there before winter sports became common for both sexes.

Climbing brought these women into contact with nature in

a new way... It gave them an excitement not easily available in their middle-class lives: Gertrude Bell set the foundation for her whole audacious career when she embraced the challenge of the mountains. Climbing also brought the possibility of relationships outside polite society: Isabella Bird is notable not for her mountaineering prowess, but for the freedom it gave her.[51]

(Virginia Woolf reminds us that Gertrude Bell – later to be identified with the vast open spaces of the Arabian desert – was not permitted to walk alone down Piccadilly until she was 27 years old.[52])

The Ladies' Alpine Club and the Ladies' Scottish Climbing Club sought to establish women's right to access to the Alps in the face of male opposition, but it was the First World War which, in transforming people's perceptions about what women could achieve, gave them full access. In Britain, women climbers formed the Pinnacle Club in 1921.[53] The new spirit, which coincided with the movement to encourage physical education and games in girls' schools,[54] was well caught in the first novel in Elsie Oxenham's Swiss quartet, *The Two Form-Captains*, which appeared in 1921. The schoolgirl Tazy boards with two boys who invite her to walk with them from the Dorf up to the Platz, where both their mother and Tazy's are patients in a sanatorium. 'She'll never do it,' scoffs another lad, who lazily plans to take the *funiculaire*. Tazy, of course, manages the two-hour climb up through the pinewoods with ease. Oxenham notes her sense of freedom: though she must take a hat with her, Tazy walks bare-headed, 'her hair ruffled by the breeze'; and she walks unchaperoned with two boy chums. Oxenham also captures the sense of *discovery*, of wonder and distance, which inspired so much 'mountain literature':

From the valley many [mountains] were invisible, others

mere white mounds above the lower cliffs. But as she mounted they grew in size and number; snow-fields glistened in the sun; glaciers could be recognised; more and more peaks came into view; and the seven-peaked range, and the great sentinels above the pass, towered aloft in almost unimaginable splendour.[55]

The scene is convincingly depicted in the novel's striking dustwrapper by one of children's literature's greatest illustrators, Percy Tarrant.

Generations of male *alpinistes* have claimed to have been inspired by the writings of John Ruskin (*Sesame and Lilies*, 1865) and Leslie Stephen (*The Playground of Europe*, 1871). I suspect that the influence of Elsie Oxenham and Elinor Brent-Dyer on generations of female readers through their Alpine novels has been comparable. In choosing to locate their fictional schools in the Alps, Oxenham and Brent-Dyer not only capitalised on a beautiful and exotic location which caught the imagination of their schoolgirl readers, but symbolically claimed the mountains for women. For girls brought up in the belief that women's place was in the home, who envisaged no place for themselves beyond the limits of the suburban street or village, these Alpine settings had a significance that extended beyond the merely picturesque. They represented in a graphic way everything that had been out of women's reach: wide open spaces, rather than the narrow women's world; remoteness; lofty heights to aspire to (Brent-Dyer's repeated 'I will lift up mine eyes to the hills' in the Chalet books): a widening of horizons in every sense.

Similarly, in the case of Oxenham's most famous location, the Abbey, a masculine stronghold is taken and appropriated for women. The Abbey is left to Joan; it stands in the grounds of the Hall, which also, unusually, belongs to a woman, Joy. Jen and her friends dance – yes, *dance* – on the cloister garth, in an obviously symbolic act of claiming the territory for themselves. So the freedom we associate with Joy and Jen in *The Abbey Girls Again*, and the other young heroines of these post-school books, goes beyond a mere absence of restriction, to an actual extension of feminine space, an encroachment on masculine power. Even when they marry (which they nearly all do), they manage to keep their autonomy *and* their space. Joy's husband, for example, comes to live in *her* home; so does Dimsie's.

Staking women's claims

Girls and women have always known that the full fantasy contained in the story-book pages will never come our way, even if we consciously covet the characters' wealth, family or gracious living in manor or castle. Still, however tangential to reality, the images are important. As Dorothy Watson says: 'We are all suckers for stories. . . . Through them we construct our image of the world around us, its rules and roles, its taboos and rewards. . . we learn to create an acceptable self.'[56]

It follows that one of the attractions for young people of girls' school stories must surely be the portrayal of characters just a little older than themselves, but not yet of their parents' generation. This age group has always functioned as role models for adolescents. In the stories of Elsie Oxenham, Dorita Fairlie Bruce and Elinor Brent-Dyer, the 'young and free' heroines who have left school but not yet married claim their economic independence, freedom from parental control, emotional maturity and their own physical and emotional space. In a world where education, law and convention conspired to keep women with clipped wings in domestic cages, financially dependent under patriarchal control, these four elements were not bad ideas for young readers to be exposed to.

In most women's fiction, Dorothy Watson points out, 'women are bombarded with negative images. . . the essential basic premise is that of the passive princess awaiting her awakening by the active prince'.[57] Yet whether the novels of Oxenham, Bruce or Brent-Dyer end in heterosexual romance or not, no one can say of the heroines that they are 'passive princesses' awaiting their 'active prince'. This message – that women have a right to be 'free' and in control of their money, space and destiny – helped equip adolescent readers to resist the worst constraints of femininity, and to sustain women in their sense of self in adult life.

2 Love and Marriage

Inevitably, after their brief period of freedom, most school-story heroines fall into line, and marry. In the novels of Elsie Oxenham, Dorita Fairlie Bruce and Elinor Brent-Dyer, romance, marriage and motherhood occur along an inexorable continuum: they cannot be separated into independent categories, for in these books romance leads inevitably to marriage and marriage as inevitably to motherhood. In this our authors reflect their times, of course. 'Love and marriage go together like a horse and carriage,' ran the popular song, and few questioned the ideology which located married women's proper role in childbearing and rearing. Indeed, so strong was the pressure to reproduce that childless couples were, until recently, assumed to have 'something wrong' with one or other partner. Living together outside marriage did not become common in Britain until the late 1960s and unmarried parenting not till the following decade. Even today, while both are perfectly acceptable in some quarters, among other people and in other places they continue to be stigmatised, while marriage and motherhood remain the 'normal' destiny for women.

In depicting romance, marriage and motherhood as inevitable for their heroines, our authors demonstrated their compliance with this ideology. None of these three women ever married, however, or, so far as we know, bore children; certainly they raised none. We have no way of finding out their experience of love affairs. But, even if they had loved and lost, children's literature would hardly have been the place to use their own experiences as the basis for a story-line. This is because children's fiction had its own conventions on these matters which, born of the moral reticence of the Victorian middle class, came to exist as a separate regulatory framework out of which few writers dared to step. These conventions were so fixed and so well known that readers tend to take them for granted. They may give rise to amused correspondence in the fanzines but rarely to surprise or incomprehension, at least not after the first encounter, however distant from our own ways of thinking they may seem.

Literary conventions

The first rule is that relationships between schoolgirls and schoolboys need to be kept at the level of 'chums'. In all these stories, with few exceptions, it is the intense same-sex relationships which are approved, and heterosexual 'silliness' is sternly condemned. For example:

> Miss Braithwaite rejoiced in frank friendships between her girls and the boys, friendships based on the comradeship and competition of work and sports, and was willing that they should have opportunity for these in their games together. But Gerda's premature attempts at flirting were as objectionable to her as they were ridiculous, and her comments and advice were scathing.[1]

Where young women are unwittingly exposed to sexualised behaviour, they find it repugnant. Oxenham's fifteen-year-old Biddy goes to a party with her college friends, male and female, and is forced to come home early because

> 'I was uncomfortable all the time. They played games, and – and I hated it! I like games at parties. I used to at school. But this was different. They were rough and – and not nice!' She

had no words in which to describe the circle in which she had found herself and the shock her innate refinement had suffered.[2]

This is in stark contrast to the contemporary teenage novel with its focus on heterosexual romance; and in contrast, too, to the modern school-story parodies such as the St Trinian's books and films, deliberately (hetero)sexualised for a sophisticated audience heavily influenced by the psychoanalytic 'truth' that the only healthy direction for female emotions is towards men.

Many factors help to explain this complete reversal of attitude. Perhaps the most important has been the steadily increasing involvement of patriarchal forces in children's literature at every level, from production to critical reception. It was once a genre left alone to develop itself, the only requirement being that it found a market, which in turn meant that it must pander to that market – hence, no hint of heterosexual sex lest the school, Sunday school or parental purchaser be offended. But children's books no longer exist in a happy vacuum. Forced to compete with magazines, television and the media generally, all dominated by the masculine values of big business, books now play a relatively small part in girls' socialisation, but one which must be seen to be all of a piece with the wider ideologies around woman's role: as independent thinker and worker, certainly, and friend to other women and nurturer of children, but, ultimately and primarily, as sex object and support for men.

This is the view of women which empowers men – who would protest, of course, that publishing is market-led and that teen romances are actually what girl readers want. In so far as this is true (though it cannot account for the continuing popularity of the Chalet books, which could not be further from the teen romance), it only confirms the power of the all-pervasive imagery and ideas peddled by just about every institution in society. As Adrienne Rich has so tellingly observed, heterosexuality is truly compulsory in the late twentieth-century west.[3]

A further convention of the girls' school story, in absolute contradiction to contemporary values, is that heroines are portayed as reluctant to grow up and resistant to romance, which they characterise as 'sentimental nonsense', until 'the real thing' arrives out of the blue, and 'changes everything'. Love is often instantaneous on the man's part, a spontaneous attraction unfounded in any detailed knowledge of the person:

> To Paul Ozanne it seemed as if he had loved Elizabeth from the first moment ... In Elizabeth Temple his ideals were fulfilled; and, almost on the spot, he had made up his mind that she, and none other, should be his wife.[4]

Women take longer to recognise love, and have to be brought around to the man's way of thinking: 'I don't want him to be an idiot and think of silly things!' Jen protests about Kenneth. 'I'm *not* a real grown-up yet, and I don't want to be.'[5] But then something happens, the scales fall from their eyes, they throw off all childish reservations and embrace love and marriage completely, realising 'how much they really cared' and how they now want 'to be taken care of'. Society's wishful denial of adolescent sexuality here combines with the powerful myth which lures so many women into marriage (in many cases, to be disappointed later) – that of love's transformative power: the idea that you become a different person, mature and wise, in a different world, secure and looked after by 'your' man.

Heroines only ever fall in love with one man: the one they subsequently marry. There is usually only one on the scene, which simplifies matters, but in the minority of cases where there are two, then only one is *really* suitable. The reader knows from the start that Jen is going to marry Kenneth – no one in her right mind would choose Dick[6] – and that Maid is meant for Jock, not for Donald.[7] If the spurned one is halfway acceptable, he gets to marry one of the heroine's friends: so Donald comes back for Belinda,[8] and Jim Hughes, spurned by Dimsie, is given Dimsie's friend Rosamund for a consolation prize.[9] Or else he's just been playing round, like Oxenham's Rex Courtney, who 'really' wants Lisabel and not her friend Rena, leaving Rena for the man who 'really' wants her, his brother Rufus.[10]

So where in real life a woman might have a series of boy-friends, fall in and out of love, be attracted to wholly unsuitable men and bored by childhood boy chums, in love with two men at once or prefer women, nothing like this was depicted in a story for girls at the time our three authors were writing – and it *could not be*. One minute the Abbey girls, described as 'tomboys' at 21, are having pillow fights and making apple-pie beds for each other and the next minute they are struck down by something resembling a religious conversion:

> 'Some day Selma will wake up to what love really means, and then they will be very happy. For her age, her attitude is right and natural; the boy must wait till she is ready to give him more.'

Some pages later:

> 'Surely she's very young for that sort of thing?'
> 'Very young; but it's the real thing, in her case. . . . Last night she had a bad fright about him, and she realised how much she cared.'[11]

Another convention is that motherhood must follow not longer than a year after marriage, though, of course, not less than nine months. Pregnancy is rarely directly announced, though it may be hinted at in a variety of more or less picturesque ways (the heroine is 'going to be busy soon' or 'isn't going out just now' or is wearing loose clothes or knitting little white garments) – or else the baby arrives without anyone having realised, apparently, that it was on the way. Mothers, at least in the novels of Oxenham and Brent-Dyer, must bear well over the national average number of children, closely spaced, and with very little trouble at the birth or subsequently. The achievement of Brent-Dyer's Jo Maynard, with eleven children including a set of triplets and two sets of twins, is only outshone by that of Oxenham's Rosamund, who has two sets of twins in one year.

Perhaps more interesting than the conventions which tell the author what to say are those which decree what she must *not* say. There are no divorces in these books, no domestic violence, no extramarital affairs or pre-marital pregnancies. Even in the books written in the 1950s no one takes to drink or drugs or struggles with depression or mental illness. All the children turn out more or less all right; there may be some problems with Joy's Margaret and Jo's Margot but nothing suggesting real delinquency. The absurdity of these conventions places a straitjacket on the writer which makes it difficult for her account even to approach realism.

We can make a fair guess at the reasons for such conventions. These kinds of children's books were identified as conservative (i.e. supportive of the status quo) and 'safe' to buy without risk of conflict with the values of wider society. Teachers and librarians, the main critics of children's fiction, were cast in a strongly moral mode, concerned to encourage 'standards' in sexual behaviour and stability in family life. Schools, churches and parents, the paying market for school stories, might well have withdrawn their support from books which offered alternative moral visions to the accepted Christian message of love within marriage and women's central role in the family. The result was that, with very few critics of the ideals of marriage and motherhood between the 1920s and the 1960s, children's literature had almost an educational and religious duty to offer positive models of wives and mothers (and husbands and fathers, for that matter) to their readers.

And the writers themselves must have wanted the best for their heroines. It would have been tragic, not to say out of character, for Dimsie to have taken up with a rotter, and if Brent-Dyer's Jo had been allowed to carry out her youthful threat of never marrying, that would have made an old maid of her for the remaining 46 books of the Chalet series. In view of the publishers' reluctance to carry the series past Jo's schooldays anyway, the author plainly could not do this to her. Not only would reader-identification be lost, but the crucial role of grown-up characters in producing the next generation of girl heroines would have disappeared also.

For all these reasons it seems to me a little unfair of Mary Cadogan and Patricia Craig to be so scathing about the 'growing-up' books of the girls' school-story writers. Comparing the genre of light romantic fiction unfavourably with school stories in terms of 'vigour, literary worth [and] psychological plausibility', they conclude that 'to palm off on a bright but inexperienced child material which has been devised to satisfy the taste of a lazy-minded or retarded adult readership [i.e. the readership of romantic fiction] is to be guilty of a serious failure of imagination'.[12] I think this is perhaps a misreading of a literary device which was never intended to be 'realistic'. Not only were authors restricted by the expectations of their publishers and their market but, because they were writing within a particular genre, there were guidelines – conventions – they had to follow. Just as writers of boys' thrillers knew the value of the end-of-chapter cliff-hanger, so writers of growing-up stories for girls accepted that a 'happy ending' meant a heterosexual romance. These elements were almost inevitably stylised but, precisely for that reason, were easily recognisable by readers accustomed to the genre and accepted as an essential element in that kind of story. That said, I would argue that our three authors were good and interesting writers who still managed to make something of their material even as they unfailingly observed the conventions. Sometimes, indeed, they surprised us.

Romance

Romantic love may have a much shorter history than marriage and motherhood but it certainly has a more extensive literature. The romance (in the sense of the heterosexual love story) has been called the women's genre *par excellence* though, till recently, this description was generally tendered pejoratively. Romances have been condemned as 'pornography for women' and opposed to all the ideals of feminism and, at the same time, have been claimed as '*the* feminist art form, as they are written by and for, and read by, women'.[13] Jay Dixon goes further, arguing in her study of Mills & Boon novels that the underlying message of the romance is that men must change to meet women's standards. Mills & Boon heroines are not prepared to take their men as they are, with all their masculine imperfections; they seek to transform them, and by succeeding in civilising them demonstrate the power of women's love.[14]

Are these 'growing-up' stories of Elsie Oxenham, Dorita Fairlie Bruce and Elinor Brent-Dyer romances in this sense? Eva Löfgren, the authority on Dorita Fairlie Bruce, thinks not. The British school story often incorporates elements from the family and the mystery story, she says, and of course the career story (see Chapter 5), but 'hardly ever from love romance'.[15] In a literal sense she is probably right, for the books are rarely concerned enough with men's characters to wish to change them. But the message that men need taking in hand by women comes through loud and clear. 'Of course, he isn't good enough for Joy, but then no man ever is good enough for a woman you like,' Oxenham's Biddy says of Joy's first husband, Andrew Marchwood.[16] And Bruce's decision to marry off Erica Innes to Derrick Gordon does not meet with Dimsie's approval either: 'He's not good enough for Erica.' Her former headmistress, Miss Yorke, agrees:

'But he is the right man for her, all the same. Erica would not be happy unless she were the managing director; and Derrick, well-directed, will become a much more satisfactory person than he has shown himself in the past.'

This is perhaps the nearest we get to the Mills & Boon model, but it is not the preferred one of schoolgirl literature. 'I'm glad I'm not marrying a man to bring him up,' Dimsie declares; and certainly her choice, Peter Gilmour, seems unusually civilised and egalitarian.[17]

As in the Mills & Boon romances, men are often portrayed as 'other' by girls' school-story writers, as of course they were in these worlds of women. Colonel Black's enforced attendance at a school assembly in the wartime novel *The Chalet School Goes to It* (1941) is a deliberately amusing example of this, where Brent-Dyer makes it plain that the blunt tool of masculine authority is no match for women's subtler powers. First upstaged by Jo Maynard and her triplet babies, he then fails to make the impression he seeks and, feeling 'like a fish out of water', concludes that everyone must be laughing at him.[18]

Men are repeatedly shown to lack women's perceptions. Brent-Dyer's Jack Maynard confesses that neither he nor his brother-in-law Jem Russell has noticed whether Phoebe Wychcote is specially interested in Dr Peters. 'You are all men. I don't suppose you *would* see,' Jo comments tartly.[19] There are many occasions in girls' school-story literature where women have to intervene to salvage a woman friend's love affair because the man has misunderstood or failed to grasp the situation. Mary Devine tackles Andrew Marchwood;[20] Dimsie

Maitland puts Kenneth Orde right;[21] Jo Bettany shames Donal O'Hara into action.[22] Bruce's heroines in particular embody a higher morality which gives them a strong crusading streak, and this in turn enables Dimsie to combat Kenneth's loss of faith at the same time as she reconciles him to Pamela, and Nancy (with a little help from an air raid) to overturn Gordon Macrae's pacifism.[23]

Caught midway between the demands of the girls' school story with its abhorrence of 'sentimental tosh' and those of the adult romance with its concern that the heroine gets the hero, our authors could not dwell too long on the love story itself. This accounts for the way in which romantic attachments occur in inexplicable or at least unexplained fashion, all attempts at analysis being suppressed. Most girls in love want to talk about it endlessly with their friends. Not so the Abbey girls: when Cicely is deciding how she feels about Dick Everett, Miss Newcastle warns the others: 'You are faced with a difficult and delicate situation, in which the only possible course is to do nothing, say nothing, see and hear nothing!'[24] But Oxenham is unusual in letting us see her heroines through the eyes of the men who (then or subsequently) love them; and though she does this in the most simplistic way, her descriptions carry conviction for the reason that she too is in love with her heroines, and enjoys nothing more than to depict them through the appreciative eyes of a bystander. 'Her momentary pause gave him his first sight of her,' runs the caption to the frontispiece illustration of *Queen of the Abbey Girls* (1926), showing Jen against the picturesque backdrop of the Abbey, as seen by Ken Marchwood, the man she will one day marry. This technique of temporary identification with the men gives Oxenham an excuse to write in unselfconscious appreciation of the women: 'How graceful she was as she moved about the room giving dainty touches here and there…'[25]

With Brent-Dyer, too, silence often shrouds the subject of

love, and even of engagements and marriages. This is indicative perhaps of some kind of middle-class notion of 'delicacy' about what could or could not be discussed. Here is Heather Raphael discussing with Janie Lucy the many engagements and marriages which pepper the pages of *Janie of La Rochelle* (1932):

'I simply loathe the idea of it. Cesca is lost to us; Rose *will* be; Lal is gone; and you are settled. Now you talk of Con. I think it's all horrible.'

'Nonsense,' [says Janie]. 'You'll be following the crowd in a few years' time, and then you'll wonder what on earth you made all this fuss about. And don't talk as if we were all dead and buried! It's most unpleasant to hear you! And don't say such things to other people. We understand, but they mightn't.'[26]

The reference to married women seeming to be 'dead and buried' suggests that poor Heather perceives them as lost to their women friends. *Janie of La Rochelle* is one of Brent-Dyer's rare excursions into the romance genre. Replete with platitudinous and embarrassing love scenes ('What she read in his eager face completed what his pleading had begun. ... Now, she knew that Rex Willoughly was the only man to whom she could ever trust herself'),[27] this novel prompted Brent-Dyer's biographer, Helen McClelland, to write:

With the best will in the world, *Janie of La Rochelle* could not be described as a very good book, even when every allowance is made for its type and period. Described in one review as 'a love idyll', it is not a genuine adult book nor yet a children's story, but hovers uneasily between the two...[28]

Quite sensibly, in the circumstances, Brent-Dyer usually avoided engaging with romance in any but the most superficial way. In *The Chalet School in the Oberland* (1954) her brave attempt to describe an unsuitable romance (Elma Conroy and the older man) falls rather flat. This is the only Chalet book to focus on the finishing school and Brent-Dyer's decision to revert to younger heroines in subsequent volumes can only be seen as the right one, so inept is her treatment of these older girls in their pathetic rebellion against extraordinarily strict regulations. Dealing only with younger teenagers, she can keep them in almost total innocence: 'I'd a lot rather win the Junior Tennis Championship next summer than go streeling round to dances with boys,' declares Judy Willoughby in *Adrienne and the Chalet School* (1965).[29] Only misfit Joan Baker, condemned for her 'cheap' values,[30] and, at the other extreme, Len Maynard, a heroine so well approved that Brent-Dyer bestowed her own nickname on her, get to enjoy romantic interludes; but Len's engagement to Dr Reg Entwistle in the closing pages of *Prefects at the Chalet School* (1970), when she is still Head Girl, vies for risibility with the engagement of Grizel Cochrane to another doctor in *The Chalet School Reunion* (1963). Of the latter, however, it must be said that the love story of an embittered 40-year-old Old Girl is a pretty unusual plot line for a girls' school story.

Dorita Fairlie Bruce wrote more romances than Elinor Brent-Dyer and carried them off with more style. Her method of dealing with the demands of the genre was to invest her love stories with a little gentle irony which, of course, divests them of much of their power. *Dimsie Grows Up* (1924) was her first exercise in this vein, in which her heroine, untouched by love, struggles to understand her friend Pam, who is enmeshed in it:

'There's something very much the matter – I wonder if she can possibly be in love. Oh, dear! these are the tiresome sort of things that happen when one grows up, and I can't help her because I haven't got any experience. I suppose they will all be doing it soon...'[31]

Later, Dimsie's anxiety turns to impatience: 'What's the use of learning to be sensible at school if it all goes to the winds directly we leave?'[32] When Peter Gilmour declares his love for her, she is horrified:

> 'You know I don't want people to be tiresome and fall in love with me. It always leads to trouble sooner or later. I have enjoyed being friends with you so much, and never dreamt you would ever want to be anything else. I'm quite sure it's just imagination; you may fancy you're in love with me, but you aren't really – you can't be – because you've always been so sensible before.'[33]

Only when another man proposes to her does Dimsie wake up to her true feelings. She tells Jim Hughes that she has decided to marry Peter Gilmour: 'No – he doesn't know it yet, but he will soon, I'm just going to find him and tell him. Why don't you go and propose to Rosamund instead?'[34] This conclusion defies the usual notion of female passivity in romance, and the hint of humour guards against bathos – though the reader may feel some indignation on Rosamund's behalf, particularly as she does end up marrying the man Dimsie rejects.

In treating the topic with humour, Bruce makes it difficult for the reader to take romantic love seriously. In *The Serendipity Shop* (1947) Julia Lendrum, noting her sister's eagerness to go sailing with handsome Perry Boyd, observes wryly to her cat:

> 'I don't suppose many people are as keen on sailing as I am; but I'm hanged if I'd go out in an open sailing-boat on a November afternoon, with the temperature at freezing-point. To be in love must have a very exhilarating effect on one's circulation.'[35]

Elsie Oxenham's earliest Abbey books shared this tone, but the later ones are excruciatingly earnest. Dorita Fairlie Bruce specialised in robust, plain-speaking heroines who give the impression that marriage cannot rob them of individuality and independence: it can only add a new, extra dimension to their lives.

Sexual attraction

Almost twenty years after her spirited condemnation of the romance in *You're a Brick, Angela!*, quoted above, Mary Cadogan published *And Then Their Hearts Stood Still: an exuberant look at romantic fiction past and present* (1994). Here she makes a more positive assessment of romantic fiction than in the earlier book, since this was intended as a celebration of the form. Though largely concerned with novels for adults she does mention in passing the three great exponents of the girls' school story:

> In Britain, home-grown heroines who grew up virtually by public demand were erstwhile schoolgirl characters who had adorned the addictive, long-running series by Elsie Jeanette Oxenham (Joy Shirley and the other 'Abbey School' girls); by Dorita Fairlie Bruce (Dimsie and the Anti-Soppists from the Jane Willard); and by Elinor Brent-Dyer (Joey Bettany and other inmates of the Chalet School).

But this time Cadogan does not classify these growing-up books as romances:

> although almost all these characters married and produced children, readers were permitted few insights into the intimacies of their lives with their husbands. (To have spied into Joy's or Dimsie's bedroom, would have seemed sacrilegious.)[36]

Two things are interesting about this judgement. One is that Oxenham, at least, *did* regard her novels as romances: several of the books from the 1930s are subtitled 'A Romance of the Abbey Girls'. And the other is that Cadogan is not quite right when she says we don't get to spy into the heroines' bedrooms. We do, both literally and metaphorically – though I am not convinced that spying into the bedrooms of married characters is necessarily characteristic of the romance. What Oxenham does do is allow us a glimpse of her characters' sexual feelings, though because she is careful to observe the convention of indirectness about such matters, readers have to read between the lines.

What characterises Oxenham's treatment of sexual feelings is that even in scenes which concern a particular heroine's awakening to heterosexual love the focus is always on the dynamics between the women characters, not the woman and the man. Take, for example, the scene where we see into Joy Shirley's bedroom, on the eve of her first wedding day.[37] Here Joy's decision to let her teenage adopted daughter Maidlin share her bed for the very last time is used to work out the emotional relationships among the four young women in the house: Jen, deprived of her last bedtime powwow with her dearest friend; Maidlin, whose heart is breaking because Joy is leaving home; schoolgirl Rosamund, who loves Joy as much as Maidlin does, but is shut out from their exclusive bond; and Joy herself, who seems not in the slightest bit nervous or apprehensive about her forthcoming encounter with the sexual side of marriage. The husband-to-be is irrelevant in this drama, except in so far as he is the cause of Joy's departure and the breaking up of the cosy all-female household.

We gain insight into Joy's (hetero)sexual feelings in a later book in the series when, after years of widowhood, she falls in love with the man who will become her second husband. There is a remarkable scene in *Joy's New Adventure* (1935) where Maidlin, arriving home from a Camp Fire meeting, bursts into the room where Joy is entertaining her suitor, Sir Ivor Quellyn. Maid, now in her early twenties, lets her cloak fall in her embarrassment and stands before them in the Indian gown which is the Camp Fire uniform.

> With her big black eyes full of shy dismay and flaming colour in her cheeks, she was a vivid picture, enough to startle any man.
> Sir Ivor's face showed plainly that he enjoyed the surprise. But before he could speak, Joy's voice rang out:
> 'Maidlin! You did it on purpose! Go to bed at once!'[38]

The sentence 'Sir Ivor's face showed plainly that he enjoyed the surprise' always strikes me as unpleasant, hinting, as it does, at a masculine sexuality which is gratified by objectifying an innocent young woman. But Oxenham offers no criticism of the distress caused to the person objectified or the conflict set up between the two women; in the follow-up scene we see Ivor and Joy sorting things out between them but ignoring Maidlin, who, confused and rejected, runs away from home. Joy's jealousy and thoughtless behaviour are presented as arising naturally from her character, and we forgive her, as does Maid, when she explains:

> 'I never thought any man could wake me up again. I thought all that was over for me; that side of me was dead. I thought I was happy enough with the children, and you, and Jen. But I was only asleep, and Ivor woke me, and I found I didn't belong to myself – or to Andrew [her first husband] – any more.'[39]

That Maidlin has been sacrificed in the process is passed over. She has lost both Joy (her dearest love, who by her own admission no longer 'belongs to' her women friends, and her own innocence. She has been cast not simply as a sexual object, existing for men to gawp at uncensured, but as an active agent in her own objectification, blamed by Joy for her lover's sexualised response even when she was unaware, uninterested, even appalled by it. Oxenham justifies this little rite of passage for Maidlin in terms of the greater good of Joy's happiness and subsequent marriage. Readers can comfort themselves in the face of Maidlin's inevitable pain with the realisation that the prize of marriage will one day be offered to her, too – which will presumably make it all worthwhile. Though not fully developed, then, this curious incident does have more of the ring of truth about it than most romantic developments in these books.

Oxenham does actually refer to sexual relations between a man and woman on one occasion, albeit obliquely and, of course, within marriage. The occasion is a telephone call from Rosamund to Joy and Maid the morning after her wedding. Rosamund has married an older man who has been disabled all his life. No one ever expected Geoffrey to marry and he was generally assumed to be incapable of fathering children. The Abbey girls, indeed, are dubious about Rosamund's choice of husband (even though he *is* an earl), since they fear she may be deprived of children and, though this is not explicitly mentioned, of 'normal' sexual relations. But Rosamund has invested a good deal of energy in seeking out new treatments for the man she loves, and after the wedding night she is able to announce triumphantly that they are 'both very happy, and very pleased with one another'.[40] It doesn't take much reading between the lines to understand this as referring to Geoffrey's success in bed.

On their return from honeymoon Rosamund assures Maidlin that the doctor sees 'no reason why he shouldn't lead an absolutely normal life in every way'. 'That proves you were right to marry him,' says Maid; to which Rosamund replies, 'I'll prove it more fully yet!'[41]

Sure enough, nine months later Viscount Verriton is born.

As we have seen, Brent-Dyer never touched on sex; even her love scenes are perfunctory in the extreme. But Bruce's *Wild Goose Quest* (1945) must be considered in this context, since it represents Bruce's most serious attempt to write a romance, probably (as Sheila Ray has convincingly argued) originally with an adult readership in mind.[42] There are two romances: one between assertive Katharine Raeside and absent-minded Adam Farquhar, in which she capitulates the moment he displays an unexpected masterful streak; and one between Colin Raeside, a doctor, and a stranger who has lost her memory. What is disconcerting about Colin's attachment to 'April' is that he plainly prefers her to have no past and no identity. 'She seems perfectly happy as she is,' he declares. It is not clear whether Bruce was aware of the sinister implications of this attitude, which lends credence to the feminist argument that heterosexual relations are so constructed in our society as to encourage men to objectify and depersonalise women. But she permits a woman character to challenge Colin: 'How can she be perfectly happy without the foggiest idea as to who she really is or where she comes from?'[43] And, indeed, the author alerts us to April's precarious mental state with an authorial aside that 'beyond these pleasant pastures stood that sinister door to which she had no key, and behind which any horror might be lurking to shatter all her present joy'.[44]

When that horror appears, it is at least half Colin's fault. An incident jogs her memory, sending her into a panic. Colin rushes not simply to comfort her but to declare his love, demonstrating a crass lack of concern for anyone's feelings but his own: 'Oh, April, darling, darling!' he cries. 'Forget the dreadful things altogether. . . .I love you with all my heart and soul, and I will let no harm come near you if you will only give yourself to me.' True to the conventions of children's literature – and doubtless Bruce's personal morality – he is careful to add: 'Marry me, and I will take care of your future.'[45]

April responds to these words with understandable distress:

'Please don't!' she cried half-incoherently, pushing him from her with all the strength she possessed. 'I – I thought at least I was safe with you, and now – oh, I can't bear it! Where am I to go? And what can I do?'[46]

He has the grace to apologise immediately, but the fact remains that he has inexcusably taken advantage of her vulnerability. Woman-like, however, she takes responsibility for what has happened: 'There is some reason – one of many things I cannot remember – which makes me shrink from any love-making.'[47]

Boundaries are clearly not Colin's strong point, for we next see him pulling rank as a doctor to impose his will on poor compliant April. Just as she begins to recover her memory, Colin forestalls further revelations by sending her to bed with a sedative. This helps to spin out the story, but also makes him master of the situation.

It turns out that April – really Ailsa – had married a rogue who deserted her on her wedding day, after she had made over her entire fortune to him. Luckily, however, after he abandoned her in a lonely spot in the west of Scotland and flew off in his plane with his mistress, he crashed, killing them both. Ailsa is thus free (and surprisingly keen in the circumstances) to accept Colin's proposal of marriage. A braver author than Bruce would have allowed Ailsa to send Colin away to grow up a little and reflect on his immaturity in wishing to marry a blank slate for wife.

Wild Goose Quest is regarded as something of an anomaly in Bruce's oeuvre, possibly because it fails both as a story for girls and as an adult romance. Its attempt to depict love realistically violates the conventions of writing for girls (and disappoints our expectations of a lighter touch), while the ending slips right back into them (the easy, unproblematic solution of marriage) in a manner unacceptable to an adult audience. I would argue, however, that it demonstrates Bruce's imperfect mastery of the adult genre rather than an expression of her personal views. The real message of Bruce's work – and Oxenham's and Brent-Dyer's – lies beneath the surface.

Love for women

In the Victorian world of separate spheres, love, as an emotion, belonged in the feminine sphere, the sphere of feeling which men could not handle, and was therefore more easily expressed in relationships between and among women than in the context of heterosexual romance. Shereen Benjamin notes that even when Brent-Dyer is telling a courtship story, the love that is being described is the love between two women friends.

> When, for example, Juliet arrives back at the school after her time at college to find that the boyfriend who has jilted her is staying at the Kron Prinz Karl, an emotional scene is enacted, not between her and the young man, but between her and Joey. In a moving episode, Juliet is persuaded to confide in Jo, and Jo responds with declarations of love for Juliet: 'I love you,' Jo said softly. 'Love brings understanding.' When, thanks to Joey's intervention, Juliet becomes engaged, no such scene is enacted between the engaged couple.[48]

Even if it was a convention then that openly expressed heterosexual love should be kept off the pages of literature for young women, the unambiguous message received by readers is that 'the real emotional work and investment takes place between girls and women, with men providing a distracting and irritating sideline'.

The same focus dominates Elsie Oxenham's books. Mary Devine's loving intervention secures Joy Shirley's engagement, even as Mary struggles with what in other contexts would be recognised as a broken heart as a result of Joy's hurtful treatment of her:

> Mary sat staring at the letter. Then she looked up, her eyes dazed. It was as if Joy had struck her. Something she had cherished for a year died at that moment.[49]

Mary is able to draw on her own emotional experience to help Amy Prittle, a young woman from her London office who is so devoted to her that when Mary moves to the Abbey she takes a post in Wycombe to be near her. After she has written to Mary, telling her how much she missed her 'and a lot of nonsense that I hardly liked to read',[50] Mary is deterred from snubbing her by her recollection of how she had felt when the Abbey girls left town. So she does for Amy what they did for her, taking her out to tea, inviting her to a dancing party and persuading her to join a dancing class. Here she makes new friends, including another of Mary's protégées, Nell Bell. Nell's fiancé died in the influenza epidemic after the First World War and she has been living in an unhealthy world of dreams ever since, imagining herself married to the dead man and keeping house for him and their children, till Mary steps in and finds her a job as nurse to real children who demand her full attention. Nell's gratitude to Mary equals Amy's, and they find common ground in their openly expressed love for the older woman – so much that, when Nell sees Kenneth Marchwood approach the Abbey girls at their party, she becomes anxious about his intentions:

> 'Here's a gentleman! Isn't he tall and handsome? But I hope he won't want to marry Miss Mary and take her away. Though I would, if I were a man.'[51]

After the media publicity surrounding the prosecution of the lesbian novel *The Well of Loneliness* in 1928, these unselfconscious expressions of women's love for women were liable to misinterpretation and condemnation, and Oxenham turned increasingly to heterosexual romance for her plots, at serious cost to realism and sincerity. But she kept the spotlight on her women characters, pushing the men off-stage as soon as they had performed their essential roles as suitor and then as father of the heroine's many children.[52]

Even Dorita Fairlie Bruce, least sentimental of the three, is on surer ground when describing the love of one young woman for another. Take a favourite character, Primula Mary Beton, for example. We first meet Prim as a new junior at Springdale in *The New House-Captain* (1928). She adores prefect Diana Stewart, initially because Di looks like her heroine, Mary, Queen of Scots, and later because a mutual attraction develops between the older girl and the unusual junior. In her first term Primula helps to mend Diana's broken friendship with her chum, Peggy Willoughby. Years later, when Prim is a prefect, Diana returns as games mistress:

> Primula...went off in the direction of the Seniors' room, but she was not to reach it just yet. Half-way down the passage she was hailed from behind by a voice which she had not heard for some time, but which was still familiar and still held its power to thrill her.[53]

This time, Prim helps to mend the broken romance between Diana and the absent-minded Professor Kersey, an archaeologist, thus bringing about Di's engagement. (Note that all three of our authors used this device.) In a letter sharing the news with a schoolfriend, Primula writes: 'Diana is going about looking frightfully happy and lovelier than ever. I can't help feeling,' she concludes with a touch of envy, 'that Professor Kersey is an extremely lucky man.'[54] This is not a very different sentiment from Nell Bell's remark that, had she been a man, she would have wanted to marry Mary Devine.

In *Dimsie Carries On* (1946), set in the Second World War,

Bruce manoeuvres for Primula almost to fall in love with the naval lieutenant destined for her best friend Anne Willoughby. Fortunately she realises what is happening and, with uncharacteristic humility, checks her feelings:

> 'Good old Anne!' she said aloud. 'So that's how the land lies, is it? Well, I am glad I found it out in time, before I had gone too far to pull up. ... Do you presume to think any man would think twice about you who had the least chance of falling in love with old Anne?'[55]

Yet Primula's relationship at this time with her superior officer in the Wrens, Antoinette ('Tony') Semple, is much more vividly conveyed, the attraction not simply spoken about (as is her feeling for Robin Burnett) but emerging with memorable clarity from the conversations and interactions between the characters.

Our final encounter with Primula Mary Beton takes place in one of Dorita Fairlie Bruce's last novels, *The Bartle Bequest* (1955), when she comes to Colmskirk as curator of its new museum. The Colmskirk novels are all romances, so Prim gets her man at last – but on what terms! In competition for the job she beats the young man in question, Tim Nisbet, but once in the post she proceeds to demonstrate gullibility in trusting an agent who supplies her with fake antiques, and lack of expertise in not detecting them. Tim Nisbet, of course, *does* recognise and trace the fakes. So what can she do? She resigns to marry him, and he gets her job.

> 'Now, I understand, he will take over the Museum from Primula as soon as they are married, and though he will be the official custodian, she will always be at hand to help him ... Colmskirk will gain all round, and the young people be happy into the bargain; and Primula will be saved from making any more silly mistakes.'[56]

What a depressing conclusion this brings to Primula's emotional and professional development, and incidentally to Dorita Fairlie Bruce's writing career. That the 'fearless honesty' and 'purposeful' ways which so attracted Diana Stewart to the young Primula Mary in *The New House-Captain* of 1928 should give way to this cheerful acceptance of domesticity and her husband's professional superiority is a sad commentary on the postwar demands of children's literature, which decreed that the only love worth celebrating was that of a man who showed you up as a fool and took your job, in return for the gift of marriage.

For these unmarried women writers, who themselves lived largely in a world of women, the love of women friends was something they knew at first hand, something they could describe from personal experience – unlike heterosexual romance and marriage. It is this which, conventions aside, gives their portrayals of relationships between women such immediacy and texture. Here they were writing from the heart.

Marriage

Bridget Fowler observes in *The Alienated Reader* that the formula of interwar romantic stories

> confirms life-long, monogamous marriage, chosen by the partners themselves, as the setting for desire; it offers a Madonna image of women as a glorified wife-mother role and it represents the private sphere as the only context for unalienated existence.[57]

Girls' school stories of the same period certainly affirm marriage as the setting for desire, however indirectly. But school-story heroines who marry rarely fit the 'Madonna' image, and marriage is not presented as the only context for unalienated existence: other contexts are available both for wives and for spinsters.

Marriage is idealised in the novels of Elsie Oxenham, Dorita Fairlie Bruce and Elinor Brent-Dyer. In the Chalet books, for example, when Grizel tells Miss Carthew she can't imagine ever marrying, the mistress tells her not to worry about it till it comes,

> ' – if it does. But if it does, Grizel, it's one of the ends for which God made woman. Never forget that. Madame loved her school. She still loves it. But I think she would tell you that she is happier now than she ever thought she could be.'[58]

Pamela in Bruce's *Dimsie, Head Girl* (1925) is less convincing:

> 'I can hardly think of a single Jane Willard girl who has turned out a drone. Except, of course, the married ones. But you couldn't exactly call them drones either, could you? Housekeeping's about as big a career as any, not to mention the trouble they have to take in bringing up their children.'[59]

Bruce does not sound as if her heart is in it; yet she dutifully marries Pamela off not long after leaving school. Oxenham can be even more cynical. When injury brings Damaris' career in ballet to an end, Jen wonders what she will do with herself now. Are there any thoughts of marriage? No. 'Pity!' says Jen. 'It would solve your difficulty.'[60]

Authors had very little choice about their depiction of marriage if they wished to be published and wanted to keep their readers happy. Marriage was really the only acceptable career for girls between the 1920s and the 1960s. Becoming steadily more popular after 1921, it reached a peak in 1971, when fewer than 5 per cent of women would not marry at some point in their lives. The qualifications for marriage became less stringent: women ceased to have to choose between marriage and a career, they no longer expected their men to be single-handedly responsible for the expense of setting up home and keeping a family, and they took risks on the basis of love, knowing that, if they made a mistake, divorce was both less stigmatised and easier to obtain. Even as schooling became more serious and academic for girls it was diluted by compulsory 'home economics' or 'domestic science', imposed to reflect, but also to perpetuate, the idea that girls moved out of the family into the school and back to the family again, with scarcely a glance at the world of work and no attempt to challenge men's dominance in public life. Marriage was therefore presented in literature as the high point of feminine achievement. As Rosamund says to Maid on the occasion of the latter's engagement: 'Maid, dear, careers are all very well, . . . but you've reached out and grasped the real thing.'[61]

My feeling, however, is that where authors have idealised marriage in these novels, they have deliberately adopted an unrealistic mode so that readers will recognise it as mere deference to convention. And readers do recognise it: witness the amused but tolerant contributions in the fanzines, from girls as well as adult women, pointing out the instances of idealisation of married life in the pages of their favourite authors.[62] Brent-Dyer's biographer, Helen McClelland, observes that 'Joey, when grown-up, gradually becomes less a character than a collection of stereotypes, designed to evoke admiration.'[63] Our authors' real attitude to marriage lies behind the façade of acceptance, in the stylised depiction of the institution, the safeguards they provide for their characters who marry and the emotional interactions going on under the surface.

The safeguards first. Unlike the great majority of real brides at this time, most school-story heroines are stripped of very little power by marriage. They do not become financially dependent on their husbands, because they all have money of their own, either inherited or obtained through work. Having nurses and governesses, they are not restricted by childcare responsibilities which drain their energies and prevent them from following a vocation. Above all, they are not absorbed into *his* world, forced to abandon their own friends and interests to devote themselves to his. Benedicta, an Abbey girl who is not wealthy (and does not marry in the books), names the problem:

> 'I've often thought that marrying was more fun for the man than the girl, Maid. He gets the person he wants to live with him and take care of his house, but if she has any sort of job she has to give it all up, and her home, and everything. He doesn't.'[64]

Maidlin, who deeply resented Joy's first marriage and later confessed she had been 'glad Andrew wasn't coming back',[65] and had greeted news of Joy's second engagement with 'Oh, I wish people wouldn't do it! All this marrying – breaking up our home!',[66] is in full agreement. 'Look at Rosamund! She gives up her cottage and the life she had chosen, and starts out on a new big job, all to please Geoffrey.' Joy, of course, has *not* had to give everything up: as Maidlin notes, no doubt storing away the example, she still has her home and her friends.[67]

When Maidlin's turn comes along, she very properly presents her married role as acting as her husband's hostess:

> 'Some people get married knowing they're to be house-keeper or cook, but Jock can arrange all that for us; what he wants me to do is to keep a jolly home and welcome other people into it and make them feel we're friendly. He's never been able to invite his friends to his house, because he's never had one; he's lived in London, and it's not the same.'[68]

Leaving aside the suggestion that men cannot make a home alone, none of this largely decorative work is going to interfere with Maid's career on the concert platform or her frequent visits to the Abbey, the manor or the castle to visit her friends.

When Maid gets engaged, Joan tells Jock Robertson: 'You come before even Joy, now.' He replies: 'But Lady Joy runs me very close.'[69]

Indeed she does. On her wedding day Maid chooses to dance only with her husband, even when he offers to 'give you up to your pals for half an hour'. But she refuses: 'I can't leave him out of anything today.' The implication – and he knows it – is that on any other day she *will* leave him out, in order to return to her female circle.[70]

Marriage is welcomed at the Abbey only when it leaves intact, or more or less intact, the world of women. 'Go away! We haven't time for you, Andrew Marchwood! . . . Taking [Joy] away from us . . .' is how Joy's first fiancé is greeted;[71] and:

> 'We've all been afraid Joan would have to go off to India or somewhere with [her soldier husband's] regiment; Malta, or Egypt, or some other awful place! "Awful", because it would take her away from us.'[72]

Oxenham has two ways of dealing with alien husbands, aside from getting rid of them altogether (as she does with Andrew Marchwood) – keeping them off-stage as far as possible, or absorbing them into the world of women. Men with ordinary nine-to-five jobs would be easier to handle, but none of her heroes falls into this category; indeed, the problem with so many gentlemen of leisure is how to remove them from the domestic scene. Bill Kane, for example, planned to go into the navy, but when it appears he has inherited a large estate he thinks he'll 'go to Oxford and mess about for a year or two. I might get a degree, and again I might not! Then build a house, get married; and settle down.'

His girlfriend is unimpressed. 'And do nothing worth while, for the country or the world?'

'It's jolly well worth while!' he protests. 'Every man who makes a home and raises a family adds something to the world!'

But Patricia persuades him to stick to the navy. 'I must be able to think a lot of anybody I marry! I've no use for slackers.'[73] And of course men in the navy spend most of their time away from home.

Only rarely does Oxenham confront masculinity and expose its limitations; but when she does, her depictions are both credible and effective. Ivor Quellyn is a good example of man as 'alien'. A long-term bachelor, he comes to marriage unused to living with other people; as a man with a high-status job, he is used to getting his own way, and lacks the inter-personal skills the women take for granted.

> He understood and could handle orchestras, which, in their devotion and loyalty, never questioned his decrees; but without suspecting it he had become an autocrat. In this new home life which was such a joy to him, he was constantly coming up against the fact that people were individuals and no two were alike; he never knew how Joy or Maidlin or Jen would take things. It was not the first time he had been told he did not understand; even Gail had said he was an idiot.[74]

When he tries to get one of the girls to tell Joy the unwelcome news that he has been offered an appointment in America, Benedicta asks scornfully: 'Can't he do some of his own jobs? Do all men need to be looked after?'[75]

Elinor Brent-Dyer shares this perception of men as different, but is more respectful. Many of her male characters are set up as authority figures, powerful within their professions and at home alike. Both Jem Russell and Jack Maynard use their status as doctors to control the lives of others, including their wives, with stern diktats assisted by drugs. They are depicted as parental disciplinarians, and exercise that role, sometimes to excess. When this happens – as when Jem punishes Sybil for causing the accident to her little sister – women must step in to mediate, and to mitigate the harshness of their treatment.[76]

But there are male characters in the books of all three authors who are poles away from this masculine stereotype. We are told that Dick Bettany, for example, has always been overshadowed by his twin sister, Madge.[77] The Chalet singing master, Mr Denny, is the epitome of effeminacy, but though his manners and dress cause comment, he is as loved and respected as any other member of staff. In Oxenham's novels, the Earl of Kentisbury is depicted as the weaker partner in the marriage because of his disability and in contrast to his powerful wife, Rosamund. Kenneth Marchwood, too, with no masculine world of work to go to, fits comfortably into the world of women. Bruce's Nancy marries a clergyman, a role not noted for its heroic qualities. Nancy's comment after their first meeting is that 'he reminds me of a Newfoundland puppy, and I feel I ought to pat him and give him a biscuit'.[78]

Every school-story wife makes a show of deferring to her husband. Rosamund claims to put Geoffrey's health first, as Jen does Kenneth's when forced to undertake a world tour to hasten his recovery from an accident.[79] Joy goes to New York with Ivor. But see how these incidents are framed. Rosamund is congratulated for her sacrifice in having seven children in quick succession, apparently to secure the Kentisbury lineage in case Geoffrey should die early. Jen hates every minute of her world trip, cutting it short in desperation to get back to her children – and her women friends. Of what she and Joy see in their travels, we are told nothing. All three women actually resent their wifely duties and are pitied, and have to be praised, for making an effort.

In problematising women's role in marriage Oxenham is following a pre-twentieth-century literary convention which had its basis in the real compromises Victorian women often had to make in marriage. 'There was [for Victorian writers for girls] no question that a girl could just fall in love and then live happily ever after with a Mr Right,' Judith Rowbotham explains in her book on Victorian girls' fiction. 'This understanding of the reality of marriage meant that love was placed before girlish readers in an essentially pragmatic way.'[80] As Joy faces the first serious test of her married life – whether or not to accompany her husband to the States – Jen observes: 'You know, Maid, Joy's never really come up against what it means to be married, until now. With Andrew, her married life was all honeymoon.'[81] And 'what it means to be married' here is having to give way to your man, to move into his world – something which romantic heroines, and real-life women, assumed they should *always* do.

Eva Löfgren sees parallels with the Beauty and the Beast tale in the ugly, often disfigured men whom Dorita Fairlie Bruce's heroines choose to marry (Peter Gilmour, Kenneth Orde, Derrick Gordon). But, contrary to fairy-tale,

> The marriages of Bruce's schoolgirl heroines are often equal marriages, happy partnerships with professional implications. Miles and Charity will run the farm together.[82]

Before his marriage to Dimsie, Peter Gilmour, too, declares that: 'We'll be partners always, and I don't mind prophesying that you'll be the better healer of the two.'[83] (What a contrast to poor Primula Mary Beton's professional partnership 22 years later!) Peter is not only modest, he is refreshingly free from personal jealousy, correcting Dimsie's honest avowal that he will always come first with her:

> 'There are so many people in your world, Dimsie mine, and all with so many demands on you – and it seems to me that the one who is most in trouble will always be apt to come first with you!'[84]

Married, Dimsie conceals management skills under a veneer of wifely submission, letting her husband imagine he is boss while actually she is getting her own way.[85]

Brent-Dyer, like Bruce, prefers a certain type of tall, fair, ugly man ('Jack Maynard was ... "no film star" for looks[86]), but hers combines a teasing manner with a patriarchal will. Her description of marriage as a choice to 'see him across the breakfast table every morning of your life'[87] has a cosy, innocuous feel to it; but Brent-Dyer's husbands, though loving and generous, inhabit the public world and can do nothing for themselves in the home. When Julian Lucy needs to get to work early one day and requests breakfast at 7.30, his wife Janie says: 'It won't hurt Michelle and Bonita [the maids] to get up at six for once; and I rather like it, once I'm up.'

'Oh, but I hadn't thought of your getting up for it at that hour,' Julian says quickly (one wonders when they normally eat breakfast). 'I can pour out my coffee for myself for once in a way without coming to any harm.' But apparently he can't. 'No, thank you! I know what that would mean! Coffee-stains on the table-cloth, and everything higgledy-piggledy on the table.'[88] Youngest of the three writers, Brent-Dyer is the one with the most entrenched ideas about gender roles.

Readers of girls' school stories recognise that many of these fictional marriages are dynastic alliances designed to keep favoured characters within the inner circle. Many real people marry relatives of friends but in girls' stories this propensity is so common as to suggest a woeful lack of suitors. It ensured that one's choice of partner was of the right social class, of course: in Bruce's *Wild Goose Quest*, poor James Wildgoose is ridiculed as a possible suitor for Katharine largely because he is not,[89] though Brent-Dyer treats a similar situation much more sympathetically in *The School at the Chalet* (1925). Like all our authors Bruce preaches social egalitarianism – Tibbie Macfie's father, for example, is in the retail business, and she is embarrassed by a broad Glasgow accent her friends at

Springdale scarcely notice[90] – but when it comes to partners for her heroines, a very narrow range is actually acceptable: army officer, landed gentry, or professional alone would do. Oxenham, of course, is even more snobbish: anything less than a baronet is hardly to be countenanced, unless he be highly regarded in the arts, in which case, as with Ivor Quellyn, a knighthood could be expected to follow in due course. Oxenham likes to link up her characters to their ancestors in historical novels, a device Bruce also uses. But Bruce joins up present-day families too, with Rosamund marrying Pamela's brother and Erica, Jean's. Brent-Dyer, the most democratic of the three, also indulges in this practice, going to town with the La Rochelle connections; a family tree is needed to sort them all out.

Letters to the fanzines and attempts by other people to continue the series are evidence that readers love to match-make: imagining events after the last book in the series, they conjecture as to whether Brent-Dyer's Len will really marry Reg, as the author planned, or would Roger Richardson be a better bet? Clearly Oxenham's Margaret is destined for Andrew, and Jansy for Dickon, but who shall we team Elizabeth up with? These alliances, like the production line of babies, become in the end mere plot devices intended to keep the characters we know and love together, as rarely happens in real life.

Motherhood

The anti-feminist backlash which characterised British society between the wars, and again in the decade after the Second World War, put pressure on women to leave the workplace, focus on domestic life, and make careers of marriage and motherhood. The closure of the wartime nurseries, the exhortation for women to boost the falling birth rate, and John Bowlby's books on the need of babies and infants for a mother's *constant* care, formed a powerful combination which, together with the ideological attraction for many of a return to 'normal' home life, ensured that women's participation in the paid workforce plummeted. The popular support enjoyed by girls' school stories in this period was in large part due to a perception that they promoted traditional family values and appropriate gender roles. But in their depictions of parenting, as of marriage, these apparently conservative novels often challenged cultural norms in ways which encouraged their young readers to think beyond the usual stereotypes.

Conventional sentiments can be found, of course. Here is Gisela, former Head Girl of the Chalet School and now a wife and mother, enjoining Jo to grow up in a novel of 1931:

> 'A nation is largely what its mothers are. The wives and mothers and sisters have much to say in the moulding of men. If we are not what we ought to be, how can we expect our men to be great?'[91]

And here is the Bettany family at home in Britain in 1953:

> By [9 a.m.], the family breakfast was over and all the family were scattered – Mr Bettany to his work in the estate office; the girls to make beds, do light dusting, and see to the meals for the rest of the day; the boys to such chores as bringing in coal, coke, and logs, cleaning shoes and knives, rigging up in the laundry the lines for the week's washing, since it would be impossible to hang it outside today.[92]

Apart from Mrs Bettany's inability to 'see to the housekeeping', owing to a recent spell in hospital, this could hardly be a more correct vision of gender-appropriate behaviour within the middle class.

But one obvious challenge to convention lies in the books' inevitable focus on girls, leading to an interesting rejection of the cultural preference for boy children at this time. In these books, daughters are obviously preferred: Joy and Joan in the Abbey books, Brent-Dyer's two favourite heroines, Jo and Janie, and Bruce's Dimsie all start their families with girls. Elder brothers will not be able to crush this generation! Though Oxenham pays lip-service to the idea that boys are better – Jen is 'triumphant' when she produces twin boys – she makes it clear that Rosamund's desire for male heirs is solely for dynastic reasons; of her two sets of twins, we are told, 'the countess was secretly delighted that they were all girls'.[93]

Like all representatives of the older generation, the mothers of the original heroines are conspicuous by their absence. Dimsie's mother is actually mad at the beginning of the series; after she recovers her sanity, she provides the gentlest of foils to her strong-minded daughter in *Dimsie Grows Up* (1924), but then disappears. Joan's mother in the Abbey books takes the opposite route, declining in middle age into a 'frail, white-haired little lady'[94] not fully in command of her senses: 'she can't bear to be left alone with visitors ... She must have somebody to turn to all the time'.[95] Oxenham patronises her shamelessly – 'Mrs Shirley was installed in a corner'[96] – and then kills her off. Jen's mother, too, leans heavily on her daughter – 'I simply can't leave Mother to do everything; she gets so worried, poor dear, and it's so bad for her!'[97] – and dies young. But Oxenham's account of Jen's relationship with her mother after her father's death does have the ring of truth, for Jen comes to appreciate her mother's courage and the ties that bind them as women:

'I never quite understood her before, though I was always very fond of her. She didn't seem to sympathise in things that mattered a lot to me, or to understand how I felt.'[98]

Greater scope to develop the mother–daughter relationship emerges with the second generation, for here the mothers are established characters with personalities which already exist outside the mothering role. In any case, our authors could never have brought themselves to cut their heroines from the story completely. The presentation of fully elaborated characters who add motherhood to their repertory of achievements, rather than let the institution take them over, is perhaps the most important message these books put across to readers who, in real life, were being offered much more restricted visions.

Bruce really shows us only one of her heroines, Dimsie, as a mother. Unlike Oxenham or Brent-Dyer, Bruce does not buy into the superwoman image; she furnishes Dimsie with a realistically sized family, one girl, one boy, and, like the others, allows her to enjoy some domestic help. But as she also pursues a full-time career as herbalist and dispenser in her GP husband's practice, even contemporary readers would not fault Dimsie for employing a governess/au pair to care for her two pre-school children and the children of two of her friends. The governess, however, finds the household 'very peculiar' simply because Dimsie is not a full-time mother. Bruce's portrayal of the children is refreshingly lifelike: they are childish but also perceptive. Dimsie and her friends do not organise their lives around their children, though they clearly care about them.

The governess later reveals herself as not what she appears to be (this being wartime, she is a spy) by her unsympathetic reaction to the children – and to Dimsie:

'No wonder the children run wild if their mother is so eccentric! But one so often finds that, don't you think? with clever women who keep on their profession after marriage.'[99]

Readers immediately side with Dimsie, as they are meant to do, and take away the message that combining motherhood and a career is definitely not eccentric.

Elsie Oxenham knew next to nothing about children and, while purporting to centre her heroines' attentions on their off-spring, actually dealt very cavalierly with them. In her first novel, *Goblin Island* (1907), Marjory's parents go off to Australia because her mother has been told she can no longer live in the English climate, abandoning poor Marjory, who, because of an accident, is forced to lie flat on her back the whole time.[100] She is left to the care of another family and expected not to mope. Lisabel Courtney is quite prepared to leave her baby with her sister-in-law in England should her husband be posted to India: 'one has to put up with that sort of thing sometimes,' she says coolly.[101]

The older second-generation daughters (Jansy, Littlejan) in time become satisfactory heroines in their own right, albeit with unrealistically good relationships with their mothers:

'You can't fool about with Mother; if she says a thing she means it. You can sometimes wangle things with Aunty Joy – she's the twins' mother; but it's no use trying that game with Mother. But she's terribly nice, you know; I always like her, even when she's being really firm.'[102]

Joy's twins, the centre of their widowed mother's life for too long, retain babyish ways almost beyond readers' endurance, but even they are individuals, which is more than can be said for the long tail of the Abbey families. In the later books child-bearing degenerates into a kind of competition ('So Jandy Mac has won this winter's baby race!'[103]), and babies are presented as designer accessories long before such imagery became common:

'What a picture those three babies make together!'
'Here comes Rosamund,' said Joan. 'Now we shall add two little yellow-heads to the picture, to make it complete.'

The author's real lack of interest in these children as people is accurately conveyed in the countess's follow-up remark, addressed to her nurse: 'Dump them here with the rest; we'll call you when we've had enough of the infants.'[104]

In an era in which families of two to four children were the norm, Oxenham's habit of bestowing child after child on her heroines diminishes their credibility, and resembles nothing so much as a child with an ever-expanding collection of dolls to name and admire, as Cadogan and Craig pithily remark in *You're a Brick, Angela!*.[105] The point is, of course, that Oxenham is interested only in exploring the relationships between and among the women and older girl characters. The arrival of babies, like the intervention of men, is simply a means to that end.

Childless herself, Oxenham – like Bruce and Brent-Dyer – had little experience of the charms of infants and none of the joys of motherhood. Not only were older girls her intended audience, but she and her sister-authors were clearly happiest writing about the age group they knew from their personal interactions with the girls' organisations in which they were involved.

Though Brent-Dyer shared the 'cheaper-by-the-dozen' philosophy of family size, on the whole she treats parenthood much more seriously than Oxenham and offers some strongly felt lessons in child-rearing. Her biographer suggests that she liked to depict large, happy and intact families because she came from a broken home and her only sibling died at seventeen.[106] She accepts that mothers will be largely responsible for parenting – 'Like most men, Jack has a pathetic belief in the ability of mothers to keep their offspring in hand by sheer instinct,' Jo confides[107] – but sees an important role for fathers, too, which extends beyond the heavy hand – 'they *are* Jack's children as much as mine'[108] – and offers scope for masculine demonstrations of love and tenderness as well as discipline.[109] She is as opposed to cold strictness with children (contrasting critical Mrs Carey with her more easygoing sister Mrs Arnold in *Lorna at Wynyards*)[110] as to over-indulgence

(Emerence[111] and Zephyr,[112] for example). She demonstrates the result of capricious parenting in her portrayal of cowardly, timid Kirsty in *Jean of Storms* (1930) and the older, though very similar, Erica in *They Both Liked Dogs* (1938).

Jo Maynard's aim is to be a 'chum' to her children:

> 'I certainly don't intend to be one of those *bossy* mothers who think that they can and should order their children about as if they were so many little slaves. ... *I* think you should be as courteous to a child as you are to anyone else.'[113]

As a teenager I was never very comfortable with the idea of my mother as a 'chum', and indeed did my best to distance myself from her. This embarrassed detachment does not seem to afflict the Maynard triplets, rendering less believable, to me, the professed egalitarian mother–daughter relationship they enjoy with Jo. Jill Eckersley notes that junior members of the New Chalet Club today are not very keen on Jo as a mother: 'They felt that she had favourites and [they] didn't fancy being called "sugarpie" in public...'[114]

But Brent–Dyer successfully debunks the traditional mother image of children's literature of the time: that of the selfless figure at the centre of the home, without needs or interests of her own, catering to the every whim of husband and children.

> Jo Maynard was sitting on top of the gate at The Witchens when the car arrived. It was a most reprehensible act for anyone who was not only a wife but a mother; but it is to be feared that a good many of Jo's habits were inclined that way.[115]

She expresses a clear preference for women whose horizons are much wider than home and family, not only in her pleasure at Madge Russell's transformation in Canada, but in her description of her other favourite character, Janie Lucy, of whom Rosamund Willoughby says: 'However much she may be tied up with her own family, she always seems to be able to take in a dozen other folk at the same time.'[116] Jo Maynard is the same; and in addition Jo has her writing career.

It is possible to trace fashions in bringing up children in the pages of these books: what to feed your baby, breast versus bottle, rubber dummies, spanking, how much attention children need, and so on. One of the most interesting changes is in attitudes to adoption, today a process fraught with difficulty and hedged about with restrictions and safeguards. To Oxenham, Bruce and Brent-Dyer, adoption was as easy as pie: 'No one need go without a family.'[117] One of the most fascinating plot devices indulged in by these authors is the adoption of a child or children by a woman who is not married and is quite unconcerned about the absence of a father figure. Oxenham's Rosamund, for example, fights a legal battle to get custody of her father's baby son. (Rosamund herself had been more or less adopted by Joy, along with Maidlin.) Brent-Dyer's Madge thinks nothing of bringing young Robin into a household already swollen by teenage Juliet, to which are added (after her marriage) her brother's children and her orphaned nieces Daisy and Primula. *Jean of Storms* adopts Allison and Kirsty; Mollie Thurston (*They Both Liked Dogs*, 1938) brings up her nieces Freda and Erica, and so on.

While many purposes may be served by the child/ren's arrival, it is clear that authors often see the responsibility as a means to maturity for the young guardian. Certainly there can be few surer ways to force someone to grow up quickly than to have a child thrust upon them. But Oxenham and Brent-Dyer, childless spinsters both, take a rather idealised view of the process, seeing it as at once too easy and too successful. Emotionally immature people rarely make the best parents. Probably Madge and Rosamund will cope. They have all the confidence in the world, though Rosamund can't have much practical knowledge. Eve, however, in *The Troubles of Tazy* (1926), is quite a different case. Presented with baby Pierrot, the orphaned child of local Swiss peasants, she declares:

> 'I want someone of my own to love and work for. I want to take care of someone, and nobody needs me, except Pierrot. Nobody has ever needed me, except cats. ... I've had nothing to do but play with cats. I want to do something more than that, but you've never given me the chance. You wouldn't trust me. You never took the trouble to find out what I could do, or to teach me anything properly. I've been hungry for something real to do.'[118]

Frankly, those whose needs have not been met are doomed to disappointment if they think that children will meet them – rather, those children will prove to have exhausting needs of their own. Oxenham loses touch with reality when she offers up a baby as a cure for emotional dependence. Brent-Dyer is perhaps more realistic in *Jean of Storms*, when Jean realises that 'the old, quiet life of household duties, Guide-work, and folk-dancing, and carefree happiness was over'.[119]

Adoption is also a device for providing an unmarried woman with a child without resorting to pregnancy outside marriage, unmentionable in a girls' story. Yet here again Oxenham, in so many respects the most conservative of the three authors, proves the most interesting. In *Biddy's Secret* (1932) she offers us a baby which, though not born out of wedlock, might as well have been, for Biddy's ne'er-do-well husband leaves her soon after the birth. As a deserted wife and single mother, she feels unable to face her family or friends, and Maidlin has to pursue her to France and bring her back. Oxenham takes the easy way out and offers Biddy a second chance with the man she *really* loves, the first husband conveniently dying abroad; but at least she does not follow through with her original plan, callously voiced by Jen, to let

Biddy's sister Mary adopt the baby 'so that it shouldn't interfere with Biddy's career. I think she'd be pleased and thrilled.'[120] Instead, Biddy is revealed as a natural mother who, in contrast to some more favoured Abbey characters, recognises the drawbacks of motherhood but still wants to bring up her child herself:

> 'I was sorry about her at first; I thought she'd be a nuisance. And she will, of course. But when I saw her, Maid! . . . She's a person, a new person, come to be company for me. She'll be in the way, but she's my own, and she'll be worth it.'[121]

Biddy's Secret can be read as a forerunner of the modern unmarried-mother novels such as Josephine Kamm's bleak *Young Mother* of 1965, which I first took to be a career novel for girls, only to find that the heroine is forced (typically for the time) to give up her baby for adoption, or Margaret Drabble's more challenging *The Millstone* of the same year, whose heroine rejects this solution.

A contributor to *The Abbey Chronicle* once suggested that when Joy cuts off her hair before her marriage to Ivor, the action symbolises the end of an era: 'The friendships which had filled her life inevitably receded', which this reader regretted.[122] But though Oxenham's focus certainly shifted from Joy to the younger characters, primarily in response to pressure from her publishers, I think the married heroines continue to inhabit a world of women, their post-wedding life being little different from their 'young and free' period or indeed their schooldays in this respect. This is most true of Oxenham's novels – Brent-Dyer's men are more interventionist, and we see little of Bruce's heroines after marriage – but to some extent it can be said to characterise all the growing-up novels. Moreover, although heterosexual romance is presented as the goal of all school-story heroines, the depictions of love between women friends, both before and after marriage, are stronger, more realistic, and more memorable.

This world of women is illustrated by Rosalind's comment when she and Maribel turn up for tea with Jen Marchwood and find Kenneth there: 'Gosh! We'd forgotten there was a husband!'[123] So has the reader...

3 Old Maids

There are two heroines in Dorita Fairlie Bruce's novel *Triffeny* (1950), seventeen-year-old Triffeny and her great-aunt, Miss Tryphena Blair. At the story's start Triffeny appears as a likeable but shallow young person, something of a problem to the adults concerned with her welfare (like so many girls' story heroines, she is an orphan). Her aunt, however, is altogether more striking.

> In her youth Miss Blair had been a beauty and she still carried herself with a slight – and quite unconscious – arrogance which gave an air of distinction to her leisurely movements; for she was never known to hurry. Even now, when she was approaching fifty, that remembered beauty had not faded, only mellowed into something yet more attractive. She was slim and erect, with masses of thick black hair hardly touched with grey, and a complexion which by contrast was almost startlingly fair. And she had a gracious charm of manner which carried with it its own welcome. People were always pleased to see Miss Blair and she accepted her popularity with simple enjoyment.[1]

This very positive portrayal of a middle-aged spinster is reinforced when Triffeny, brought into her orbit, grows to love, respect and model herself upon her independent aunt. The turning point is reached when she rejects an offer to work for a bigger firm out of 'love – love of you [Miss Blair], and of Blairhill... I just know I could never leave you nor go away from here.'[2]

I first read this book when I was 23, and at that age I hardly noticed anything out of the ordinary in the characterisation or focus. It has a good story, I thought, and it's as well written as Bruce's novels usually are. Then I read it again 20 years later. I was immediately struck by the fact that here was a book for girls that placed the spotlight on a woman character who was neither young nor married, who ran her own business and played the role of mentor to a young niece – an interesting variation on the usual father–son tradition.

Then, just as I was congratulating myself on locating a strong, attractive Old Maid character in girls' literature, Dorita Fairlie Bruce did something dreadful to Miss Blair. She killed her off in Chapter 20.

What are we to make of this? Granted, the death was necessary to Bruce's plot (Miss Blair has to die to enable Triffeny to step into her shoes), granted even that she was writing for girls who would naturally expect her to prioritise youth, there is a double message here which indicates a fundamental ambivalence on Bruce's part. On the one hand Miss Blair is positive, attractive, central, in control – on the other, she is dead by the end of the book. Moreover, she dies of heart disease, prompting the reader to ponder the cause. We are told it was a congenital weakness, but it could just as easily have been caused by stress or overwork. Is this what happens to women who try to run businesses as if they were men? Would she have survived if she had lived a 'proper' woman's life of marriage and motherhood? What is Bruce trying to tell us?

Reading this novel at 23, I saw only another adult's early death, a familiar enough device (as we saw in Chapter 1) to clear space for the heroine to spread her wings. Reading it again at 45, I found Miss Blair's death extremely painful. For I, the reader, was by then an old maid of similar age; I had admired the character and had come to identify with her, rather than with the childish heroine.

What adds a further layer of complexity is that we know

that Dorita Fairlie Bruce, too, was an old maid when she wrote this novel – indeed, she was substantially older than her fictional old maid, for Bruce was 65 in 1950, when the book came out. What must it have felt like to kill off a character who was sixteen years younger than herself?

There are hints of ambivalence throughout the novel. Bruce constantly reminds us that Miss Blair does not look her age. Triffeny says, for example:

> 'One can't think of Great-Aunt Tryphena as "old". Why, she's far younger than that dried up stick of a Phena [another niece]! She has such a lovely colour, and no lines on her face except where everyone ought to have them – those laughter crinkles at the corners of her eyes. ... She's only about forty-nine, and you can't call that so very old.'[3]

Nor does she act 'old'. Triffeny's friend Julia tells Miss Blair, 'You're one of those people who have been born young, and young you'll be to the day you die.' Irritatingly, instead of resenting the comparison, 'Miss Blair coloured with pleasure at the girl's compliment.'[4]

In both instances, Bruce is buying into a cultural preference for youthfulness when she could have spoken up for experience. As Barbara Macdonald has pointed out, when a woman accepts a compliment like this, 'she has to join in your rejection of [other] old women'.[5] The only thing wrong with being old is other people's ideas about what that means, but it is hard to resist complicity. Anyone who feels flattered by being taken to be younger than she really is embarks on the slippery slope of distancing herself from reality, which is so harmful to our sense of integrity and self-worth. Cynthia Rich has written:

> We attempt, of course, to avoid the oppressor's hateful distortion of our identity... But meanwhile, our true identity, never acted out, can lose its substance, its meaning, even for

ourselves. Denial to the outside world and relief at its success ('Very few people think of me as old as I am'...) blurs into denial to self ('I'm always surprised [at the hairdresser's] when I look down and see all that gray hair because I don't feel gray-headed').[6]

In the 1970s and 1980s radical feminists encouraged women to reclaim words which had been used against them, like 'hag' and 'crone', for that would take the sting out of them: likewise, if you are happy to call yourself old, age cannot be held against you. But of course Dorita Fairlie Bruce was writing half a century ago and within a particular ideology; and many will feel that it would be absurd to expect her to choose the conservative medium of children's literature in which to challenge it.

On the other hand, simply by depicting these largely all-women worlds with their purposeful, businesslike heroines, Bruce was out of step with the message of the postwar years that women were to retreat to the home and submerge themselves in family life. In the circumstances, then, she did very well to paint as positive a picture as she did of the older single life when it is clear that, in writing a book for publication, she found herself caught in a double bind. She had a story to tell, which demanded strong single heroines, but she wrote for a living, which meant she had to observe the literary and social conventions of the time.

Ninety-nine per cent of novels published for girls in the early part of this century, including most of those by Elsie Oxenham and Elinor Brent-Dyer, presented youth and marriage in a favourable light while marginalising or ignoring old and unmarried people. Yet the authors who wrote these books were themselves neither young nor married. They were single and, by the standards of the time, old. And they were women. Old maids. One could hardly sink lower in the scale of social esteem.

Viewed in this light, Dorita Fairlie Bruce's *Triffeny* does offer some resistance to the dominant ideology. The plot is not a standard romance story-line. Miss Blair plays a leading role for two-thirds of the book and there is no masculine love interest or pressure to marry. (Julia Lendrum does have a sort of boyfriend, Sandy Lamond, but their relationship, while businesslike and recreational, is entirely free of sentimentality; Julia, again challenging the rules of romance, clearly has the upper hand.) Even if, as readers, we are meant to identify with young Triffeny – as I suppose her intended audience would have done – the girl's growing admiration for her aunt leads us to share her response. In a genre focused on youth and heterosexual love, in a society which regarded women as secondary, the unmarried as superfluous and the old as useless, Miss Blair is actually quite a remarkable creation.

The spinster and her problems...

I have called this chapter 'Old Maids' in an effort to reclaim an expression which has been used in a pejorative sense for 200 years, though it has rather fallen out of use in modern times. In nineteenth-century Britain it had a very precise meaning: it referred to older, unmarried, middle-class women (or 'ladies'), and it carried with it connotations of failure and dependence. In a society premised on the notion of marriage as every girl's destiny, spinsterhood was not seen as a choice, even though some women then, as now, deliberately chose it.[7] 'It is often said that the true vocation of woman is marriage,' a journalist wrote in 1872, 'and this is something more than an opinion: woman, in the minds of those who take their ideal from the past, *means* a wife, or a sister of charity.'[8] The sentiment expressed here survived well into my lifetime and is, I am sure, alive and well today in some quarters: the idea that, however successful, good or happy a woman may be, if she does not get herself a husband along the way, she is not a real woman.

In the second half of the nineteenth century considerable

concern was felt about the large proportion of women (close to one in four) who 'failed' to marry. The emergent feminist movement took advantage of this tide of unsupported spinsters to press for education and job opportunities for women so that they could support themselves. The result was that, preferring careers to married dependence, the number of single women continued to increase past the turn of the century, which, together with the wholesale slaughter of young men in the Great War, brought the proportion of unmarried adult women to a high point of 37 per cent in the census of 1921.[9]

The early years of the twentieth century were therefore good years for spinsters, in so far as unmarried women stood higher in public esteem than ever before. There were such a lot of them, and many were making names for themselves in careers or in public life. Some, like Florence Nightingale (who died in 1910), were household names. Since only very exceptional women were able (or indeed allowed) to combine a career with marriage, the great majority had to make a choice that is unimaginable nowadays; and though marriage was always considered to be the superior role, sufficient numbers opted for the career for the status of *all* single women to be raised. A former principal of Cheltenham Ladies' College, Lilian Faithfull, wrote in her autobiography of 1924:

I think there can be little doubt that indirectly the higher education of women discouraged marriage in so far as it gave to women an alternative which had none of the dullness or limitations of home life, and much of the variety and opportunity for initiative and energy which would not normally be found in domesticity.[10]

In 1921 Elsie Oxenham was 41, Dorita Fairlie Bruce 36 and Elinor Brent-Dyer 27. Brent-Dyer alone could fairly claim that she was of the generation who lost their potential mates in the war, though there is no evidence of any real attachment. When war broke out Oxenham was 34 and Bruce 29 so both were already old maids according to the standards of the time. Moreover, they had probably absorbed the conventional Victorian attitude to spinsterhood unpalliated by any feminist critique of marriage such as that offered by Mona Caird in *The Morality of Marriage* (1897) or Cicely Hamilton in *Marriage as a Trade* (1909).

Immediately after the First World War the granting of the vote and other reforms favourable to women, such as the Sex Disqualification (Removal) Act of 1919 and an equalising Divorce Act of 1923, gave way to a backlash against independent women. Disguised as society's wish to 'return to normalcy', the economic and ideological pressure on women to marry and withdraw to the home quickly became intense. Deirdre Beddoe writes in her history of women between the wars:

> In the interwar years only one desirable image was held up to women by all the mainstream agencies – that of the housewife and mother. This single role model was presented to women to follow and all alternative roles were presented as wholly undesirable.[11]

To social and economic pressure was added a third, more powerful inducement to marry: the influence of popular psychology, which, attaining respectability in the 1920s, persuaded a gullible public that women would be emotionally and sexually incomplete if they failed to marry or, worse still, that failure to marry indicated a warped or infantile emotional and sexual development. The 'science' of sexology, hitherto grasped by only a few, now became common knowledge. Close friendships between women, and even between schoolgirls, began to be condemned as exhibiting abnormal sexual development. Girls and women should focus their energies on *men*. The successful prosecution of Radclyffe Hall's lesbian novel *The Well of Loneliness* in 1928 gave conservatives another stick with which to beat spinsters, since the tremendous publicity surrounding the case brought all single women, especially those associated with girls or other women, under suspicion of being sexually depraved.[12]

Little wonder, then, that marriage rates flew up. By 1940, 81 per cent of all women of 25 years of age were already married (the corresponding figure in 1910 had been 47 per cent). Indeed, slightly more than a quarter of all twenty-year-olds were married (the figure in 1910 was only 7 per cent),[13] lending some credibility to Elsie Oxenham's increasingly youthful brides and to Frieda's comment at the wedding of Jo's friend Simone, who must have been 22 or 23 at the time: 'So the last of our quartette is married. I am so glad. Simone is too dear and sweet to spend all her days teaching.'[14] Thus wrote Elinor Brent-Dyer, an unmarried woman of 47 who had, to date, spent all her days teaching.

We cannot therefore be surprised at the internalised self-hatred such remarks seem to indicate. It is impossible to exaggerate the viciousness of the attacks on unmarried women in the interwar years and the 1950s, often clothed in the 'scientific' language of psychological 'truth', which was far more wounding than mere prejudice or pity. Here, for example, is Laura Hutton in her attractively titled *The Single Woman and her Emotional Problems* (1935), one example of a fairly extensive literature on spinsters current at the time:

the woman deprived of a mate and denied children is bound to suffer from loneliness. ... Such loneliness is the result of the frustration of a deep instinctive need, and frustration, as the psychologists know, is only too often likely to reactivate in the adult the frustrations and conflicts of very early childhood, and these, unrecognised and indeed unconscious, produce incongruous and exaggerated emotional reactions and emotional instability, which tend to wreck any personal contacts and friendships which are achieved.[15]

Here the spinster is placed in an impossible position through the combination of persuader language (*deprived, denied, bound* to... the psychologists *know*), which skilfully removes the possibility of any different interpretation and the setting up of a 'no-win' situation which the poor woman is powerless to change, her frustrations being 'unrecognised' and indeed 'unconscious'! This would have been cheering stuff for our authors to have read! And even if they had not come across it, doubtless friends and acquaintances had, so they would have had to deal with other people's perceptions and misconceptions about their lives. Bruce was not untouched by the influence of popular psychology, and her amusing treatment of the locum headmistress in *Nancy Returns to St Bride's* (1938) who lectures the sixth-formers on 'complexes' and the unconscious may represent an attempt to get her own back:

'Sonia has a curious idea,' [Nurse] answered carefully, 'which seems to be that she is suffering from some obscure disease. She tells me they have been learning, in the psychology lectures, that it is quite possible to have some serious complaint without being aware of it.'[16]

Everything that mattered to single women – their jobs and leisure activities, friendships and community work – was grist to the psychologist's mill:

All interests rooted in sensuous pleasures... are potential channels for frustrated sexuality, such as interest in colour or design, in movement (dancing, athletics) or in music. ... There is no doubt that an immense amount of useful sublimation of sexual energy is carried out by the majority of single women.[17]

Here the dancing and music which were so precious to both Oxenham and Brent-Dyer, Oxenham's sensual enjoyment of the shapes and colours of pottery, the school–story writers' passion for games, are all dismissed as mere 'channels for frustrated sexuality' rather than useful and rewarding interests in their own right. Likewise, women's work with girls is presented by Leonora Eyles in *Unmarried but Happy* (1947) – the patronising tone of the title alone beggars belief – as a form of 'sublimation through work':

> the reproductive impulse, if natural parenthood is denied (in the case of a woman), can be diverted to the things connected with marriage and motherhood – the care of children and sick people; the care of people in homes and institutions, all of which use up the mothering instinct; the teaching of children; the making of beautiful things for human use ... Work in girls' clubs, in Girls' Guildry, ... and numerous other organisations offers some paid posts to suitable women, and many unpaid jobs for the woman with a little leisure time... [18]

Dorita Fairlie Bruce was an officer in Girls' Guildry for 33 years. Elsie Oxenham was involved with Camp Fire, another girls' organisation, and Elinor Brent-Dyer with the Guides. [19] It could not have been easy to maintain a strong sense of self-worth when your life's work was devalued in this way.

The Second World War offered new opportunities for female independence which, as we have seen, Dorita Fairlie Bruce seized on for her fictional heroines, while Brent-Dyer ran her real-life Margaret Roper School until 1948. But the postwar years brought a similar reaction to that which had followed the First World War, with the attack on independent women taking an even more extreme form. M. B. Smith announces in *The Single Woman of Today: Her Problems and Adjustment* (1951) that the book

> cannot give any adequate answers to the single woman's outstanding questions – 'Why am I to be husbandless and

childless? How can I lead this unnatural life with some measure of fulfilment?' It cannot offer to banish any of the frustrations, depressions, restlessness, which come from such a disastrous denial of a woman's natural rights to biological and psychological completion.[20]

It is not possible to read the words 'husbandless and childless' without a sense of failure or loss: once again persuader language precludes the possibility of a contented single, child-free existence. To feel thus is unacceptable: spinsterhood is 'unnatural'; spinsters cannot be 'really' fulfilled, they can have only 'some measure of fulfilment'; they are 'incomplete'; they will 'inevitably' suffer from frustrations, depressions and restlessness – and if they say they don't, you can be sure they will be told they do, only the problem is 'unconscious'. Their lives, it seems, are a disaster.

From the 1920s through to the 1950s, then, the dominant view of spinsters was negative. They were seen as neurotic, lonely, sex-starved, incomplete, unnatural women, unable to form good relationships, tending to wreck the ones they did have, and forced to substitute paid employment, community activities, art and exercise for their *proper* work in the family, which included both motherhood and (quite explicitly) heterosexual sex. Their values and achievements were undercut at every turn for, however much they meant to the individuals concerned, they were not valued by the world at large, which viewed them only as substitutes for real womanly values and achievements. Their very sense of integrity and well-being was an illusion, for single women were not whole, could not be whole, could not even be well.

The fictional stereotypes

It is safe to say that none of our three authors depicts an old maid who in any way resembles the sexologists' model –

although she can be found in adult fiction, for example Clemence Dane's unpleasant *Regiment of Women* (1917) or G. Sheila Donisthorpe's even more repellent *Loveliest of Friends!* (1931). What we tend to get in girls' stories is a collection of stereotypes, many harking back to Victorian depictions of old maids as comic, or pathetic, or both. Brent-Dyer gives us 'the Stuffer and Maria', for instance, first met on a train from Paris to Basel in *The Head Girl of the Chalet School* (1928), who later turn up at the Oberammergau passion play: 'They were elderly, clad as the Continental humorous papers invariably portray the English tourist...'.[21] In *Triffeny* Miss Blair is neatly contrasted with the kindly, ineffectual Misses Beith, Triffeny's guardians.

> The Misses Beith (daughters of the late head of the firm) always reminded him of a pair of budgerigars, fluttering and twittering about their cage.[22]

Since Triffeny is their sister's daughter, the women are unlikely to be over 60 but they act (and look, if Margaret Horder's charming illustration is to be believed) as if they were very elderly and out of step with the times. When the lawyer points out that Triffeny should be trained for a career even if, financially, there is no necessity for her to work for a living, Miss Caroline observes:

> 'But what difference would it make in the end? Merran Lendrum has married, just like anybody else. ... They may be as modern as they like, but it invariably comes to that in the long run – doesn't it, Kate?'
> 'Of course!' maintained Miss Catherine, apparently regardless of the fact that it had not done so in her own case or Caroline's.[23]

What lends a discordant note to this gentle irony – for Bruce is clearly making fun of the sisters – is our knowledge that the author, too, consistently espoused similar views about marriage in her writing, while remaining unmarried herself.

In a later Colmskirk novel, *The Debatable Mound* (1953), Bruce capitulates by marrying off an apparently confirmed middle-aged spinster in the concluding pages of the novel. Cousin Pen (Miss Pennycuick) actually has the choice of two potential husbands, and decides to marry her late cousin's widower, Professor Crawford, rather than the poor Admiral, who has been assiduously courting her throughout the book. Both men are presented as figures of fun, unable to cope in any worldly sense (though both, of course, have reached the pinnacle of success in their respective professions), and one wonders why any woman would bother with either of them. But Miss Pennycuick declares:

> 'I can't think of Cuthbert living down there alone, with no one to mend his socks and air his undervests. He would be such a helpless sort of creature with no woman to look after him; and I know I should just be worrying about him all the time.'[24]

Another well-tried image of spinsterhood is that of the 'character'. A good example of this is Elinor Brent-Dyer's Auntie M, Miss Merrill Chudleigh, great-aunt to the eight young Chudleighs of *Chudleigh Hold* (published in 1954, but probably written earlier).

> 'They've a great-aunt living with them who's a tremendous sport. She says and does the maddest things, and they never know what she's going to do next. It makes life rather hectic, so Gill says.'[25]

Chudleigh Hold was one of Brent-Dyer's earliest excursions into the thriller genre. It involves an impostor cousin – a German girl (betraying the book's wartime origins) – whose cultural difference is used to point up the very British respect shown by the young people towards their elderly aunt and the different, though still sincere, respect accorded Miss Chudleigh's companion, Miss Molesley. This is demonstrated in a scene where the 'cousin' expresses a wish to occupy a certain bedroom, which Miss Chudleigh wants for her companion. Asks the impostor: 'You will give this old aunt what she asks?' 'Of course. Anyhow, Auntie M. never asks – she takes for granted as you may have noticed by her letter.' The German, who has her own reasons for desiring that particular room, demurs: 'But – after all, I am a Chudleigh – one of yourselves. Why should this servant-person be considered before me?'[26]

A subtle hierarchy of age and class is revealed here. To the Chudleighs, Miss Molesley isn't exactly a 'servant' because she is a 'lady', but one in reduced circumstances, forced to take a position as paid companion. The respect due to her is the courtesy one must extend to a family retainer who is almost of one's own class. Miss Molesley is 49 – old enough to be an old maid, but not elderly. Miss Chudleigh is in her seventies, but age does not disqualify her from respect because she has money of her own. She also has a forceful personality, but of course this personality is only acceptable – is, indeed, only possible – because of her wealth. Miss Molesley's personality also derives from her financial position. She is 'colourless' and passive because she is poor.

Miss Molesley is another old maid stereotype, set up in contrast to Miss Chudleigh in the same way as the Misses Beith are to Miss Blair. She is described as

a mousy little lady, clad in well-worn blue serge with a toque-like hat sitting on string-coloured locks drawn firmly back from a face that could never have aspired to ordinary good looks, even in its best days.[27]

The daughter of 'a poor and elderly vicar and his equally poor and elderly wife', who both died when she was nineteen, Agatha Moseley 'had had to turn out into a bleak world to earn her own living, without friends or relations to help her'. She drifted 'from one unsatisfactory post to another for over twenty years, never able to save'. Then, after a long period of unemployment, she obtained the position with Miss Chudleigh. From that point on, her financial problems were at an end: she was 'well-housed, well-fed, and well-paid, and treated with a consideration that was new to her'.[28] This description, hinting at the horrors and indignities which could be attached to a lady-companion's life, seems old-fashioned even considering that it was probably written in the early 1940s and not in 1954, when the book was actually published. The Victorian lady-companion was a familiar figure, but even Brent-Dyer grew up with the realisation that she would have to work, however middle class her background, so Miss Molesley's catapulting into 'a bleak world' with neither skills nor useful connections came close to anachronism even then. That her parents were elderly when she was born further emphasised the Victorianness of the portrayal. Brent-Dyer invariably preferred her parents to be young and believed that the children of 'elderly parents' inevitably experienced problems in growing up (Eustacia of *Eustacia Goes to the Chalet School*, 1930, for example, and Zephyr Burthill in *Jo to the Rescue*, 1945).

No matter how pleasant her conditions of work, Miss Molesley has to put up with the fact that 'Miss Chudleigh was an alarming old lady... her ways were not those to be expected of a lady in the seventies, and she would brook no denial of her whims.'[29] One such whim is to force her poor companion to get a permanent wave and have all her teeth extracted, to be replaced with false ones, in the interests of improving her appearance and hence her *joie de vivre*.

Having been brought up to believe that we ought to be content with the looks our Maker has given us, Miss Molesley had gone with a guilty conscience, especially when she found out the cost; but go she must, since she dared not gainsay Miss Chudleigh.[30]

Miss Chudleigh also encourages her to wear 'slacks', or at least to raise the hemlines of her skirts, and to do 'physical jerks'. She even tries to make her smoke. 'They're not poisonous, you know,' declares Miss Chudleigh. 'I'll tell you what it is, if you had ten cigarettes a day, a cocktail or two before dinner and a good five-mile walk every afternoon, it would do you all the good in the world!'[31] Even on the last page of the novel, Auntie M. is still working on Miss Molesley. 'I mean to make a very different woman of her in six months' time. Then she can begin to enjoy her life properly, poor soul. At present, she only *exists*!'[32]

The point of this is rather lost on the modern reader, to whom Miss Molesley's reservations about tobacco and alcohol seem perfectly reasonable, while many of us would fully agree with her resistance to making over her appearance to fit someone else's notion of womanly attractiveness. But Brent-Dyer was a life-long smoker and an extrovert who seems to have enjoyed life thoroughly, and she clearly identified with Miss Chudleigh's sentiments and her personality. Brent-Dyer, too, was 'larger than life'. Though domineering and insensitive, then, Miss Chudleigh is probably meant to be a positive portrayal. She exercises the 'Lord of the Manor' role that rightfully belongs to her great-nephew, buying back part of the estate which has been sold to meet debts. In a passage which must have been written when the Labour government was in power after the war she cries: 'Chudleigh Hold can't lose all that land just because a set of ninnies in the Government choose to tax the landowners so heavily to pay for their fancy ideas!' While this demonstration of Miss Chudleigh's complete identification with the values of the landed aristocracy is not surprising in itself, her assumption of the master's role is. 'Chudleigh Hold stands for more than that silly master-and-man idea. Our people and we are the same family and what hurts one, hurts all.'[33]

But, as with Bruce's Miss Blair, there is a limit to her advocacy of the single life. There is the usual dead fiancé in Miss Chudleigh's background – he died in a fall from his horse on the way to the wedding – and she unquestioningly accords a higher priority to married life. She rudely asks the girls' governess why she isn't married yet: 'A girl like you has no business to waste her time over other folks' brats when she ought to be looking after her own.'[34] And, saddest of all, by the start of the next book in the series, *Condor Crags Adventure* (also published in 1954), Miss Chudleigh is dead.

She has a gallant replacement, however, in the third Chudleigh Hold book, *Top Secret* (1955). Miss Penrose is

> 'over eighty, but doesn't look even seventy and she acts like forty most of the time. From what I've heard, she's been quite a gal from the word go! Took to New Zealand and pioneering like a good 'un. Anyhow, she made good on her own while our other two great-aunts only got married'.[35]

What Miss Penrose 'made good' at was a jam-making business she set up with a female servant. What looks at first sight like a praiseworthy instance of sisterly cooperation across the classes is on further reflection explicable in terms of the skills required for such a business: put plainly, Miss Penrose probably didn't know how to make jam and her servant did. Anyway, she made a fortune, and never married: 'says she's had no time for it'.[36]

Genre writing tends to encourage the production of 'stock' characters, and this is particularly true of this sort of juvenile thriller – not Brent-Dyer's forte, as fans will agree. And though there are plenty of examples of other stereotyped roles in school stories – the honourable schoolgirl, for example – an important reason for the popularity of the work of Elsie Oxenham, Dorita Fairlie Bruce and Elinor Brent-Dyer is precisely that they so often transcended the stereotypes which other authors relied on. The trouble with these 'character' spinsters was not so much that they didn't ring true as that they illustrated all too clearly how difficult it was to be *normal* and an old maid in a children's book – or indeed in real life, where eccentricity conferred entertainment value and deflected attention from the disadvantages of age. Barbara Macdonald sums it all up:

> This kind of response to aging is not surprising as it has always been a common response of oppressed people. It is a forced response. The midget, the court jester, the Black funny man, the fat lady, the tramp... all are responding to the oppressor who says entertain me, amuse me, deny in front of me, what I am doing to you daily. One has the moral choice to play to an audience who prefers the lie in the laugh, or to confront the oppressor with the truth that dwarfism is not funny, Black is not funny, fat is not funny, poverty and powerlessness are not funny, and old is not funny.[37]

It is unlikely that such an interpretation ever occurred to Elinor Brent-Dyer when she created her character spinsters for her young audience. But as a 60-year-old spinster, regarded as something of a 'character' herself, she would have had her own battles to fight. Fortunately, her preferred genre, and the one she succeeded best in, was the school story, which, in focusing on a community of girls and adult women (the staff), encouraged the production of many more positive old maid role models than these. So, too, did the career story, into which Brent-Dyer made one brief foray.

The female boss

One of Brent-Dyer's most prolific years was 1954. In this year she published not only the first two Chudleigh Hold novels and two additions to the Chalet School series, but also two unconnected titles, *Nesta Steps Out*, an evangelistic novel, and *Kennelmaid Nan*, an example of the career/adventure story in vogue at the time, which features a strong spinster character. When the heroine first encounters Miss Frome, the owner of Assisi Kennels,

> She saw someone who overtopped Averil's five-foot eight easily. She had a square-chinned face, handsome in a granity way, with iron-grey hair cropped like a man's and brushed back with a firmness that almost hid its slight natural wave. The most dominating feature was a pair of the bluest eyes Nan had ever seen. At the moment, they held a kindly welcome, but the girl was to find later that they could look like pieces of glinting steel. Altogether someone you could respect and rely on.[38]

The imagery here suggests another spinster 'type', the masculine-looking woman who works in a man's world and has adopted a man's style. Brent-Dyer's preference was always for tall women so Miss Frome's height does not, by itself, suggest masculinity, but the hair 'cropped like a man's' and the face which is 'handsome in a granity way' certainly do. The blue eyes which could be kindly or could glint like steel remind us of no one more than Miss Annersley, headmistress of the Chalet School, and are clearly intended to suggest business-like authority. In the 'separate spheres' world of Victorian Britain, physical and mental strength were both associated with men, physical weakness and passivity being reserved for women, though they were permitted moral strength. One legacy of these attributions was the tendency, for decades thereafter, to depict women who did not conform to feminine ideals as 'masculine' in appearance as well as character.

Miss Frome plays the mentor role to young Nan that Miss

Blair plays to Triffeny. But Miss Frome, mercifully, neither dies nor marries in the course of the novel, remaining a significant role model throughout. There is not the slightest hint of deviance, such as one might expect in an adult novel or parody of the genre, and indeed Miss Frome's conventionality rather disappoints the reader when she punishes the senior kennelmaid, Averil, for consorting with a criminal boyfriend by forcing the pair to marry!

Bruce offers a younger version of the 'masculine' spinster in Antoinette Semple, Primula Beton's superior in the Wrens in the wartime novel *Dimsie Carries On* (1946). Readers of Bruce's books would remember Tony Semple from her schooldays at the Jane Willard Foundation, where she plays an important role in *Dimsie Moves Up Again* (1922). A keen sportswoman, with 'a strong sensible face' and a short manner, Miss Semple impresses Prim with her competent authority, leading her to remark at the end of the assignment which forms the plot of *Dimsie Carries On*: 'I only hope I shall still be under Miss Semple [in future]; she's such a gentleman.'[39]

Bruce had evidently forgotten that in *Dimsie Among the Prefects* (1923) she reported Tony Semple as having married.[40] This apparent *volte-face*, which conveniently restored characters prematurely removed from the cast by marriage, was an occupational hazard for writers of long, interconnected series. Elinor Brent-Dyer married off no fewer than *three* of her Chalet School mistresses who subsequently returned, husbandless, as if nothing had happened to disturb their peaceful lives.[41]

The mistresses

This leads us to Brent-Dyer's strongest spinster characters, who are, of course, the mistresses with which she peoples her Chalet School, some of them for almost a quarter of a century. By the later books in the series, these long-serving mistresses are well into middle age and fully qualify as old maids. Miss Annersley, who claims to have been 'not much over thirty' when she assumed the headship of the Chalet School (in *The New Chalet School*, 1938), has held the post for twenty years by the end of the series, so must be over 50. Nancy Wilmot, who joined the school as a senior pupil in the same term as Miss Annersley became head, takes over from her as acting head in *Challenge for the Chalet School* (1966). Miss Annersley implies that Miss Wilmot is about 30 but a quick calculation (mathematics were never Brent-Dyer's strong point), shows that she must be around 37.[42] Brent-Dyer herself said of Hilda Annersley that she 'completely identifies herself with the School',[43] and the same is true of Miss Wilmot.

A teacher herself, Brent-Dyer demonstrated in her warmly realistic depictions of schoolmistresses the insider knowledge which was absent from the work of authors who never taught, such as Oxenham and Bruce. Characters like Miss Wilson and Miss Ferrars are among her most popular creations, and she was unusual, though not unique, in writing an entire school story from the perspective of an adult. *The New Mistress at the Chalet School* (1957) is one of her best and best-loved novels, which succeeds in making the community of grown women as attractive to young readers as the community of girls.

Miss Wilson's relationship with Miss Annersley, her co-head, is as close as that of a sister, or even spouse. In a celebrated passage when Miss Annersley lies close to death after a serious accident in *Gay from China at the Chalet School* (1944), Miss Wilson tells Jo Maynard:

'I shall never forget that awful night when she lay between life and death, and I knew quite well that no one thought she would see the morning. I knew I was very fond of her; but it wasn't till then that I realised how dearly I loved her. You've got Jack and the children, Joey; but Hilda and I are both singularly lonely people, and we mean a lot to each other. If I had lost her, I suppose I could have gone on somehow; but I'd always have felt that part of me was dead.'[44]

Miss Wilmot's relationship with a younger colleague, Kathie Ferrars, is equally intimate.

All four mistresses are presented as uniformly popular, respected, rounded and fulfilled characters for whom marriage and death are equally unthinkable. In *A World of Girls* I explored the power of these depictions, which offered girl readers the message that not only is it possible to find fulfilment in a career but that spinsterhood does not necessarily leave a woman in an emotional vacuum; she may find companionship, and even love, in the community of women around her.[45]

Mademoiselle de Lachennais, doyenne of the teaching staff, is described in *Challenge for the Chalet School* as 'a great favourite in the school. She was small and dainty, graceful in her movements, and her little dark face was full of vivacity'.[46] She is also, in her fifties, an accomplished *alpiniste* who spends her vacations scaling mountains. Miss Dene, the school secretary, whose schooldays are 'twenty years behind her', is 'a tall, good-looking woman with fair, wavy hair framing a clear-cut face'.[47] All these are positive representations with not a boyfriend, past or present, in sight; marriage simply isn't an issue – though realistically enough many other mistresses wed. It is true that Jo Maynard, in a moment of crass tactlessness, asks Rosalie Dene why she has never married: 'Hasn't there been anyone – not anyone at all?' But Rosalie, though she laughs in embarrassed fashion, responds with spirit: 'No, my love, there's never been anyone, and I don't care if there never is. I'm quite satisfied with my present life.'[48]

When writing about spinster teachers, Brent-Dyer was describing a world which not only she, but her immediate audience, knew intimately. In girls' schools up to my own schooldays, spinsters dominated the teaching profession. Looking back, women differ in their assessment of the significance of these teachers in their lives. Mary Evans says the teachers at her grammar school in the 1950s 'made themselves unacceptable to us as role models because they seemed to have rejected men'.[49] But Alison Hennegan, of the same generation, takes a very different view:

> Those women I most admired or who influenced me – Miss Fuller, my piano teacher, Miss Lacey [her mother's headmistress, who persuaded her to become a teacher rather than a hairdresser], Miss Tarrant [a university professor] – were all spinsters. Moreover, they were all women of such dignity, such presence, that they became for me the definition of spinsterhood. Very early on a word which was for others so often the cue for sniggering contempt signified for me female strength, independence and freedom.[50]

For Julia Pascal, too, grammar school in the 1960s had many irritating qualities, but it showed her 'that women could hold positions of power and authority'.[51]

The most powerful spinsters were undoubtedly the headmistresses. In a patriarchal society, authority is normally vested in men; hence the headmistress becomes, in a sense, a surrogate male figure governing her surrogate community, the school. What made this assumption of male power acceptable at the time when girls' schools were becoming more organised and professional was that the headmistress was also seen as a surrogate mother to her 'children', her pupils. This reasoning was probably the ambitious woman's passport to power in the late nineteenth and early twentieth centuries, when women's domestic role was supposed to take precedence over any career aspirations, but when large numbers of unmarried women had no homes of their own. Judith Humphrey has shown how the headmistresses of fiction 'combine absolute authority with large measures of understanding and loving kindness' – that is, 'paternal' and 'maternal' power.[52]

In real life, headmistresses exercised an important influence on their pupils (does anyone who went to a girls' school *not* remember her headmistress?), and on girls' education generally. But they were often ignored in the wider social context, since girls' education had less status than boys', and were more or less left to their own devices to exert power as they wished. Elinor Brent-Dyer, headmistress of her own school for ten years, knew this from first hand. In fictional schools, of course, the headmistress's power could be as limitless as her wisdom and personality.

Before the 1960s, headmistresses in fiction, as in real life, were almost all spinsters. In books they come in different shapes and sizes, but descriptions often focus on their eyes. Chalet readers are all familiar with Miss Annersley's keen blue eyes which never needed glasses,[53] while Bruce's Miss Yorke has 'deep-set hazel eyes, which seemed to read one through and through'.[54] Sight is a metaphor for knowledge and wisdom: the headmistress sees all, knows all, understands all. Her eyes alternately mirror her power and her compassion. Judith Humphrey points out that the religious ethos which pervades so many school stories, including those of our three authors, endows fictional headmistresses with unusual and empowering 'spiritual possibilities' including the assimilation of Christ-like qualities as heads of their communities.[55] Miss Annersley's nickname is 'the Abbess' and her Christian name is Hilda, the name of Brent-Dyer's favourite saint.

As the twentieth century progressed, the balance between the 'maternal' and 'paternal' functions of the headmistress subtly shifted in favour of the latter as girls' schools ceased to resemble large families and education became more of a business. This transition is accurately reflected in the long series of books written by all three of our authors. In Dorita Fairlie Bruce's first book, *The Senior Prefect* (1920), Miss Darrel is replaced by Miss

Yorke, whose preference for scholarship over games causes her pupils much distress. That Miss Darrel, deeply loved by her girls, is a head of the old type is demonstrated by the manner of her leaving: she has to give up her work in order to nurse the old aunt who brought her up, now suffering from a crippling illness, 'and there's no one else to look after her. I wouldn't leave you dear girls for anything but a very urgent duty.'[56] Career must give way to family obligation. There is no sense, however, that Miss Yorke is any the less loved for exercising a more professional management style.

In the Chalet books, Mademoiselle Lepattre takes over from Miss Bettany on the latter's marriage. Her leadership style is explicitly maternal; motherless schoolgirl Cornelia Flower is said to have received most of her mothering from Mademoiselle.[57] By the time Miss Annersley is promoted to the post, this kind of headmistress has become an anachronism in a large modern school. Mademoiselle is accordingly killed off and any further mothering that is needed is supplied by Jo Maynard, who is able to maintain her connection with the school largely through performing this function.[58] Brent-Dyer nevertheless emphasises the strength of the girls' feeling for Miss Annersley: as Madge Russell declares, 'I do not think there has ever been a girl in this school who knew her who did not love Miss Annersley.'[59]

In real life, women who aimed high in their teaching careers may well have struggled with a perception of female leadership as 'unfeminine'. But school-story headmistresses rarely admit to any ambivalence and their positive characterisation must have played an important part in making leadership and management skills acceptable adjuncts of women's caring qualities. For young readers, then, fictional headmistresses may have been very important role models; all the more significant because they were spinsters offering a powerfully attractive alternative to success as wife and mother.

Wise woman

For Dorita Fairlie Bruce, the most sympathetic old maid character was that of the wise woman, exemplified by the Grey Lady of *The School in the Woods* (1940). Living alone in a cottage on the edge of the eponymous woods, the Grey Lady, Marcia Johnston by name, is an author of historical romances, whose portrayal strongly hints at an *alter ego* for Bruce herself. When the schoolgirl Toby first meets her, she sees

> a strong whimsical face lit by a pair of deep-set grey eyes with humorous crinkles at the corners ... She was tall, or looked it in the long grey cloak which she wore wrapped closely round her; and her head was hatless, with thick mouse-coloured hair brushed back from a wide low brow. Her skin had the weather-beaten look of a complexion which is exposed to sun, wind, or rain alike, without fears of its washing off, or regard for its future.[60]

There are many interesting features in this description. The wrinkled, weather-beaten face suggests a pleasant acceptance of age, and there are certainly no pretensions to beauty: no heroine ever had mousy hair and a low brow! Readers know that Bruce disliked the use of make-up by girls – this features in the plot of *Dimsie Intervenes* (1937) – but here she shows that she would have adult women eschew it too, showing a healthy contempt for the cult of physical youthfulness.

That the Grey Lady (a coy appellation which many find irritating) is meant to be a sympathetic character is immediately signalled by the positive response to her of Toby's dog, Algernon. Human worth is often measured by animals in Bruce's fiction. That she is a forceful personality, unconcerned about appearances in the wider sense, is also quickly apparent. Miss Johnston delivers outspoken judgements in 'deep musical tones'.[61] Some of these are uncontentious, such as when she lectures Toby on the need to put more effort into liking 'difficult' people than those who are *not* difficult – she knows, she says, because she is one, 'but I've got good friends, thank Heaven!'[62] Here she cheerfully claims the role of outsider already indicated by the fact that she lives alone on the margins of civilisation. Other sentiments smack of eccentricity, though they are characteristic of Bruce. Miss Johnston declares, for example, that the thieves who tried to steal Dick Trevor's secret gas should get 'penal servitude for life, at the very least. But the country's grown so namby-pamby nowadays, that they'll probably be let off as first offenders, or some nonsense of that kind.'[63] This is plainly the author speaking.

Unlike Miss Blair, the Grey Lady does not die in the novel – which is either further evidence of Bruce's identification with her, or suggests a less inflexible attitude towards old maids than that which prevailed when she was writing *Triffeny* ten years later.

Elsie Oxenham's spinsters

So far Elsie Oxenham has hardly featured in this discussion. Yet arguably it was she, of these three authors, who produced the most interesting studies of spinsterhood. One reason is that Oxenham was far and away the most introspective writer, so her earlier and better work takes us inside her characters in ways that neither Bruce nor Brent-Dyer could or indeed would ever do. This greater thoughtfulness is, I think, partly the result of Oxenham's own personality (neither Bruce nor Brent-Dyer struck their contemporaries as particularly thoughtful in this sense), and partly of belonging to a slightly older generation, with different social and literary values. Oxenham was five years older than Bruce and fourteen years older than Brent-Dyer; moreover, she published her first novel in 1907, well before the First World War, while theirs date from the early 1920s. Oxenham therefore began writing before the vogue for school stories engulfed the juvenile market. Her earliest novels were not school stories; Bruce's and Brent-Dyer's earliest novels *were*, and even though their work was both formative and superior in terms of that genre, a different set of expectations and limits was imposed on it from the start.

Most importantly, Oxenham grew up with a different image of spinsterhood. Although her own life was hardly touched by the wider intellectual and feminist movements affecting single women, she must have benefited from being one of a group perceived to be pursuing worthwhile endeavours, and one which was large enough for her to feel normal, though unmarried. Certainly in her own family she would not have seemed unusual, since none of the four daughters married. And, most fortunately, she grew up with an image of spinsterhood untainted by sexology, which did not really enter the public consciousness until the 1920s. As I demonstrated in *A World of Girls*, both Bruce and Brent-Dyer had to grapple with its tenets right from their earliest novels, with Bruce's Anti-Soppist League in *Dimsie Moves Up* (1921) and Brent-Dyer's crusade against the crush in *A Head Girl's Difficulties* (1923), both scornfully reframing the common phenomenon of schoolgirl hero-worship, which had been taken for granted and even celebrated in earlier school stories.[64] But most of this modern nonsense seems to have passed Elsie Oxenham by. Her best work was produced in the 1920s and much of it seethes with the intense feeling the sexologists would have had a field day with – as critics subsequently did. And though she married off all her main heroines in accordance with the rules of the romance, she nevertheless produced a handful of spinsters whose concerns and development are as important to her readers as those of the glamorous characters centre-stage.

Oxenham's very first published novel, *Goblin Island* (1907), is narrated by a spinster daughter: Jean keeps house for her father because her mother is dead. Though only 21, as the daughter at home she has virtually no life of her own.

> Father and I were constant companions. I helped him with his work, acting as his secretary, and taking down stories from his dictation and then typewriting them. It kept me very busy, but without the work I might have been lonely.[65]

There is no romance for Jean in this book, only for her brother, and she is at her father's beck and call. 'Jean! Jean! Where are you? Are we not to have any tea to-day?' Then, after tea: 'The manuscript is ready for you now.'[66] Not a please or a thank you in sight. The book does not appear to be written in a spirit of rebellion, and indeed is said to be based on Oxenham's own experience as secretary to her father, the popular author John Oxenham.[67] The very absence of criticism is chilling. Clearly, it would have been hopeless for such a daughter-at-home to complain as no one would have acknowledged her entitlement to a grievance.

Through her involvement with the English Folk Dance Society in the 1920s Oxenham came into contact with a different kind of spinster: the woman working in a profession or in business, with her shared flat 'in Town' and her busy social life. That Oxenham was fascinated by these working 'girls', many of whom were younger than she was, is evident in her admiring descriptions of them in the early Abbey books. The Pixie, for example, was a real person, D. C. Daking, to whom she dedicated two of these books; she worked in a West End dress shop by day and taught dancing by night, and also acted as counsellor to a wide circle of friends, male and female. Neither the real nor the fictional Pixie ever married. 'I once discussed marriage with her,' remarks Miss Newcastle (another Abbey character based on a real Folk Dance Society officer), 'and she agreed, rather doubtfully, that it was the most complete life for a woman. "Yes. Yes, I suppose it is. But thank heaven it hasn't happened to me!"'[68]

These new experiences also formed the background for a much more important character in the Abbey series, Mary Devine. Mary is 30 when we first meet her in *The Abbey Girls Again* (1924), a typist in a London office, whose total lack of glamour serves only to enhance that of Oxenham's rich and attractive Jen Robins and Joy Shirley. One day Jen and Joy walk into Mary's drab, narrow, restricted life and transform it beyond recognition. They find that Mary's childhood ambition to write has been crushed by circumstances and she lives in a world of daydreams, shutting out all conflict and distress, coping less and less with reality. Jen and Joy deflect her from imminent mental illness by offering her a reality which competes with and ultimately vanquishes the daydreams. It begins with folk dancing, participation in which healthy and communal activity forces Mary to overcome her diffidence about both her appearance and her social skills. The treatment proceeds with Jen's persuading her to take on the teaching of a dancing class and Joy's inviting her to the Abbey. Installed there as Joy's secretary and companion, a successful writer at last, Mary achieves an outcome which really does rival the most ambitious of daydreams.

Through Jen's move to a home of her own and Joy's comings and goings, Mary is always there. She never marries, not so much because she is too old (Joy is no older when she marries for the second time, and Brent-Dyer has some even later weddings – those of Evadne and Grizel, for example), as because Mary's emotional energy remains focused on Jen and Joy. There is nothing she will not do for them or their children. This leads to her assuming the archetypal maiden aunt role on occasion: whenever a crisis looms, Mary is expected to drop everything and step into the breach. During one such drama, ten years on, Joan remarks: 'I was sorry to uproot Mary, when she had just settled down . . . But Jen needed her badly.'

'You needn't feel sorry, Joan,' Maidlin responds. 'Mary loves us all, but she worships Jen. She just lights up at the thought of going to help her.'[69]

At least Mary's services are not taken for granted. In a still later book, *A Fiddler for the Abbey* (1948), we read that 'Mary had been waiting quietly till she was needed'. 'Bless you, Mary-Dorothy Devine! Always there when we need you!' cries Cicely.[70] Mary's reward lies in the knowledge that she is centrally important to the Abbey girls: they depend on her as much as she depends on them. The presentation of this character reflects the ambivalence which surrounded the role of spinster until relatively recently. On the one hand, Mary's needs are almost always subordinated to those of her married friends and their children, though occasionally she is allowed to put her writing first. On the other, in Mary, Oxenham created a character whose psychology and emotional growth are explored across several books in detail quite disproportionate to her apparent insignificance as a middle-aged spinster. Mary is ever present, right to the end of the series. Though slow to reach emotional maturity, once she achieves it she soon outstrips Joy, at least, in that area, becoming confidante and adviser to her friends as well as to the younger Rosamund and Maidlin. It is Mary who, included in all family discussions, finally persuades Joy to let Rosamund leave home:

> Mary came to look, and stood with her hand on Joy's shoulder. She was several years older than Joy, and there was something protective and almost motherly in the warning pressure of her hand.[71]

In return, we are told, 'Joy will trust anything to Mary, even Elizabeth and Margaret [Joy's small daughters].'[72] Many readers would, if forced to choose, prefer to live Mary's life to Jen's, Joy's or Rosamund's, for readers know the real-life demands of motherhood which Oxenham evades. Mary is the grown-ups' closest friend and retains that significant role throughout the series. Her love for her 'fairy godmothers' Jen and Joy outshines any heterosexual romance in all the Abbey books and demonstrates that, for Oxenham, however much she might bow to literary conventions about love and marriage, the *real* relationships were those between and among women. This recognition alone makes Mary Devine one of Oxenham's most significant contributions to children's literature.

Readers might have expected our three authors to be as negative about old maids in their novels for young people as the society they lived in was about real-life spinsters. It is easier to write within a powerful ideology and deny the contradictions with your own life than to challenge it – especially if you need to make a living. In fact, all three did sometimes use damaging stereotypes, such as the ineffectual maiden aunt and the eccentric 'character,' and uncritically accepted society's preference for youth. They were not above killing off elderly characters in order to make way for the younger generation, deemed – implicitly or explicitly – more attractive. Admiring the white gown Rachel wears when showing visitors round the Abbey, Jen tells her: 'You look very pretty.... Your Aunt Ann [Rachel's recently deceased predecessor] made me think of a little old black rag-bag.'[73]

But girls' school stories also provided a splendid opportunity to feature positive role models in their casts of spinster mistresses who, as Juliet Gosling has observed of the Chalet staff, 'are not teaching because they cannot attract a partner, but as an alternative or as a prelude to a relationship'.[74] It seems likely that Bruce identified with the Grey Lady, Brent-Dyer viewed Miss Annersley as the headmistress she would like to have been, and Oxenham must have seen a little of herself in Mary Devine, the daydreaming secretary freed by her love for glamorous Joy and Jen – a love Oxenham undoubtedly shared. These characters were, in a sense, their authors' salvation, for they reinforced their sense of reality; their knowledge that single lives can be lived with dignity and pride. Through them girls received the important message that every woman has a right to personal fulfilment and that there are other roles for women besides servicing men and bringing up children.

4 Community

In *The Abbey Girls Again* (1924), Joy explains to Mary why she not only fills her life with good works – her rest home for tired girls in business, her treats for disabled children, her classes for the villagers – but also takes an interest in people like Mary.

> 'It's the feeling of responsibility, the need to share one's good things, I suppose. I know I'd feel an awful slacker if I sat down and enjoyed my house and my friends and my money, and kept them all for myself and my own little circle.'[1]

Readers of Oxenham's books, and also Brent-Dyer's and Bruce's, are presented with a positive model of a female community which exists in some cases alongside the heterosexual world and in some cases apparently independent of it. It extends beyond family to include friends, and wider social networks. Married heroines like the Abbey girls slip in and out of each domain but the books mostly focus on the world of women. Unmarried women may live entirely in this world, content in their self-sufficiency and enjoying some degree of social esteem and recognition for their work with girls or young women.

Oxenham was able to unite the Victorian notion of separate spheres from her own childhood with the 1920s movements open to girls and women. Girls moved easily from the society of other girls to a society of women, in their leisure-time pursuits, in their domestic circle, and often at work too. There was no disjuncture and no abrupt refocusing on men; if men did enter their world, it was only in the role of suitor or husband, central for a limited period and (certainly as far as

Oxenham was concerned) largely tangential thereafter.

For those women who did not acquire husbands, even less transition was necessary. These were the women who lived in a 'hostel for working girls' such as Pernel and Doranne, or a 'girls' hotel' such as St Mary's on the Platz; or else they shared a flat 'in Town', like the Pixie, who rented the top floor of a large house in Theobald's Row together with 'Brown', a typist, and 'Parr', who was in the Women's Police.[2] For the young readers who read the books at the time they were published, this must have reflected a reality which they could choose to emulate. Though there was pressure to marry and return to the private, domestic world in the 1920s and 1930s, these books showed that alternatives were available to those who did not do so – that women in this position were able to establish useful and valued niches for themselves, and that they hung on to them for some time in the face of mounting public opposition to communities of women without men.

For readers of later generations, like myself, the reality was different. All-female communities had become attenuated and devalued, if not actually obliterated; single-sex schools were under attack (shortly after I left my high school in 1967 it became co-educational); and girls' organisations had fallen into decline. It was partly because school stories offered such powerful visions of communities without men that they were condemned by critics in the 'swinging sixties' as irrelevant anachronisms. But for some of us, these books served as a haven from the pressures and prejudices of the mixed-sex world we were forced to negotiate, and became an inspiration throughout our adult lives.

From the school to the world outside

Girls' school stories are as much concerned with community as they are with individual development. The boarding school they purport to depict is, above all, a self-contained community of girls and women, and this aspect of the books has always been of particular appeal to those readers (a majority) who attended day schools. All school stories necessarily focus on the pleasures and difficulties of learning to live with other people. As Jo Maynard tells new girl Lavender,

'the only way to live with other people happily is to make allowances for them and their ideas. We all think differently on lots of subjects, and it's quite likely that other people are just as much right as you may be.'

She goes on to instruct Lavender to 'stand on your own two feet, and not go rushing off to someone every time something happens that you don't quite like'; and, finally,

'to remember that you aren't the only pebble on the beach. The school has nearly two hundred pupils now. There are the staff, too. It's impossible to let all that crowd do as each one likes. You've got to fit in with the majority.'[3]

In the series of Elsie Oxenham, Dorita Fairlie Bruce and Elinor Brent-Dyer, not only the lessons learned from this process but also the friendships themselves are carried into adulthood. Ideals inculcated in childhood underpin the behaviour of members of the adult communities. Sheila Ray has remarked, noting how older girls are taught responsibility for younger girls, and how everyone learns concern for those less fortunate than themselves, that 'Brent-Dyer cannot be faulted in providing role models for girls which might encourage them to grow into caring, well-adjusted and responsible members of the community'.[4] The same is true of Bruce and Oxenham.

Though other communities come to replace the school, very often the link with the school continues: Dimsie returns to be the headmistress's secretary, the Hamlet Club continues to meet at the Abbey, Jo lives next door to the Chalet School. Many characters become teachers and are restored to the school community in a different capacity. The adult communities, like the youthful ones, are largely all-female. As Gillian Avery observes in *Childhood's Pattern*, not altogether approvingly, 'The husbands, if there are any, count for little beside the support that the closely-knit circle of girls gives to each other.'[5] In an era when ideological forces were pushing women back into the nuclear family, encouraging them to focus their energies, aspirations and loyalties upon husband, home and children, school-story writers kept alive the connections between women, and between women and girls.

These authors opted to swim against the tide because they were all products of the Victorian and Edwardian middle class when 'separate spheres' was still the ruling principle for social life and interests. Moreover, all three were unmarried and part of a generation which included large numbers of unmarried women. Such women inevitably associated with each other in their leisure hours. In *Women Like Us*, a series of oral history interviews with older women, Eleanor describes how she attended a Women's Evening Institute after she left school: 'It was a club, we were all women together, did everything together – holidays, swimming, netball.'[6] Single women were encouraged to devote their 'maternal' energies to working with girls' organisations. Thus, Brent-Dyer was a Guider, Dorita Fairlie Bruce was prominent in Girls' Guildry, and Elsie Oxenham ran a Camp Fire for six years. Their books reflect the reality of their own lives. In Oxenham's *The Troubles of Tazy* (1926), the protagonists include a Guide Lieutenant, a Tawny Owl and three Camp Fire members.[7] In the Abbey books, Maid runs a Camp Fire, Joy is Captain to the local Rangers and Rosamund teaches country dancing to the Guides.[8]

The school story was an old-fashioned genre by comparison with, say, the new women's magazines of the interwar period, and espoused the sorts of values that made it ideal for school and Sunday School prizes. It was also a relatively unimportant genre in the eyes of the critics, for concern about children's reading did not become a social issue until the mid-1930s. For these reasons, no one noticed that school stories presented a feminine world that was very much at odds with the prevailing domestic ideology. Avoiding mixed-sex issues altogether was the preferred attitude in children's literature of the 1920s and although romance took ever increasing priority in the ensuing decades, it was not until the 'sexual revolution' of the 1960s that the movement to break up single-sex communities and prioritise heterosexual relationships won out completely. By then the classical school story was well and truly on its way out.

The community of friends

In all the series, friendships are lasting. Jo stays in touch through marriage and motherhood, though separated by national boundaries, with the other three of her school quartet – Simone, Frieda and Marie. Dimsie settles in Scotland, not far from Jean, Pam and Erica, even though they all went to school in the south of England. Several of Bruce's heroines marry into each other's families – this is also true of the Abbey girls – which further serves to bind them together. The Abbey girls remain each other's best friends. They are always there in time of need. When Maidlin sets out to find her long-lost cousins in the Lake District, for example, Jen is ready to accompany her, though this means leaving behind a husband, three small children and a number of Lady-of-the-Manor duties. Joy helps out by taking over some of Jen's tasks, chairing the Women's Institute meeting and hosting a country dance party.[9] Later, when Joy goes off to New York, the question arises as to where Maidlin should live. Jen, Joan and Rosamund all ask her to come to them. She is touched. 'I believe each one of you wants me, and it's the loveliest thing that could have happened to me.'[10]

New friendships are realistically added along the way. Nanta says to Mary Devine, 'I know you have heaps of friends, but I'd like to be one too.' Mary replies: 'One of the nice things about friends is that you can't have too many of them. There's always room for more.'[11] Likewise, Phoebe Wychcote is taken into Jo Maynard's circle in Brent-Dyer's *Jo to the Rescue* (1945). Jo tells Phoebe:

'Look at all we have – our husbands, and children, and dozens of friends, and our happy homes. If we didn't try to share, do you really think we'd deserve all we've got?'[12]

Dimsie, Bruce's most popular heroine, is depicted as someone who is constantly befriending 'lame dogs' and is completely without enemies: everyone succumbs to her charms, and her closest friends (and even her husband) resign themselves to having to share her with a wide circle.[13]

Clearly there are sound literary reasons for maintaining a constant cast of characters, to which new ones are occasionally added to offer a different perspective, but for school-story enthusiasts these characters take on a life of their own. Indeed, the very aspect of these series books which can be most off-putting to new readers – the constant references to characters we are apparently supposed to recognise, without context or explanation – is a positive pleasure for those familiar with the series. It allows us to fill in gaps in our knowledge of characters from the books we have already read. It feels just like catching up with old friends, or learning a little bit more about their past.

I have written in greater detail about the significance of friendships, both girls' and adult women's, in *A World of Girls*.[14] In this chapter I shall therefore focus on the wider area of community and the networks which help sustain contact between characters once they have left the school environment.

In particular, all three writers focus on the community provided by folk dancing, a popular club activity at the time. In the period between the wars, folk dancing was of enormous significance to both Elsie Oxenham and Elinor Brent-Dyer. Though Dorita Fairlie Bruce was not quite so interested, probably because as a Scot she had her own folk traditions, there is still plenty of country dancing in her novels and she plainly expected her readers to be familiar with the names and steps.[15] The subject of folk dancing pervades a large number of interwar school stories, important for both setting and storyline and, at a symbolic level, influencing character development. In Oxenham's books, especially, it stands as a metaphor for friendship and community.

The Hamlet Club

Perhaps the most enduring links for the Abbey girls derive from their associations with the Hamlet Club, a society for those who enjoyed rambling and country dancing. Both activities were relatively new leisure pursuits for the middle class when Oxenham began to write about them. Public concern about the countryside and urban open spaces, fast disappearing in the tide of industrial development, emerged as a force in Victorian society in the 1880s and led to the formation of such organisations as the National Trust, founded in 1895, dedicated to preserving and conserving the national heritage. Greater public access to the countryside was a complementary aim, and local walking groups were set up in various regions. But they did not come together to form an effective pressure group until 1931, when the National Council of Ramblers' Federations was set up; the Ramblers' Association followed in 1935. In the 1930s rambling was a popular recreation, but when Oxenham published *The Girls of the Hamlet Club* in 1914 it must still have been novel.

In spirit, it was in keeping with the revival of interest in Britain's folk songs and traditions that also emerged towards the end of the nineteenth century. The members of the Hamlet Club choose a queen every May Day and crown her in a ceremony involving a procession of all the former queens and plenty of country dancing. This custom, apparently common to many girls' schools, was instituted at Whitelands Training College by John Ruskin in 1881; it survives there to this day, though inevitably the college is now mixed so there are May kings as well as queens.[16]

For the Abbey girls, the fact that they were all queens in their time meant that every May Day, circumstances permitting, they return to the old school and act out the ritual of the procession and dancing. When grown-up Cicely mentions the lasting friendships she made at school, Joan points out that these are due to 'the club that takes us back for meetings, and so we keep in touch';[17] and Joy tells Biddy and Mary that 'it's only through the Hamlet Club and the President that we exist, as a crowd of friends'.[18] Later, their children are brought up in its ideals – in a world full of 'aunties'. As Mary remarks of Joy's young twins, 'When the Hamlet Club comes here [to the Abbey] to dance, the twins have dozens of aunties.'[19] The ideals are carried into new settings: when Jen leaves school at sixteen to go home to Yorkshire, she immediately decides to 'teach a Sunday School class, or get up a girls' club'.[20] In the last book in the series, *Two Queens at the Abbey* (1959), Joy's twins are set to carry on the tradition.

The significance of having once been a queen is brought home in *A Fiddler for the Abbey* (1948) when Joy's children's nurse, Beatrice, is taken ill with typhoid in New York. Joy delays her return to England to be with her until she has recovered. An acquaintance is amazed: 'And Lady Quellyn will alter all her plans for her nurse-girl?' Rosamund explains:

Beatrice is a Hamlet Club Queen, and a friend, as well as Joy's nurse. None of us could desert another Queen. You don't understand all that it means to be one of our Queens; but it's something more and closer than friendship.[21]

If this sounds like a feminine version of an Old Boys' network, it really is like that; at one point *all* the Abbey girls' nurseries are staffed by former queens, and one has the impression that they all undertook the training specifically in order to serve the Abbey girls.

At a time when Old Boys' networks determined virtually every significant position of power (even 'merit' appointments, such as those for the judiciary, drew on an extraordinarily restricted pool of candidates), this 'Old Girls' network' represented an attempt to set up a parallel power structure in the feminine sphere. In imitating the workings of patriarchy it was not, of course, what we would now regard as feminist, for there was no challenge to the principles or indeed the practical operation of patriarchy. In particular, the female version left intact an oppressive class system which permitted some members of the Hamlet Club (the Abbey girls) to assume all the leadership roles while others seemed to have existed only to service their needs in the most 'feminine' way possible: caring for their children. Oxenham clearly valued the caring role but, accepting its low status – and the reason for it – in the real world, she was careful not to confine her heroines to it.

The Hamlet Club's origins are sometimes lost sight of in the later books, but it was founded by Cicely Hobart in *The Girls of the Hamlet Club* in an effort to break down the institutionalised barriers imposed by the wealthier girls at the Wycombe school. Herself an heiress, like so many of Oxenham's heroines, Cicely aligns herself with the poorer day girls from the hamlets round about. In the end the Hamlet Club comes to the rescue of the school in an emergency and the girls are united. The very motto of the club, 'To be or not to be', is interpreted by the girls as an invitation to decide 'whether they'll just have a good time and please themselves ... or whether they'll ... care about other people, and try to do great things in the world'.[22] This is the one Oxenham novel that meets with the wholehearted approval of Mary Cadogan and Patricia Craig in *You're a Brick, Angela!*. But while welcoming the critique of class snobbery they do not comment on the other positive note that is struck by the coming together of all the girls in a common cause. Oxenham, they write,

> made much of the character-building function, as she saw it, of both the country-dancing and Camp Fire movements. Both these activities put the emphasis on group participation. One can fulfil oneself only through purposeful association with others: this debatable precept is expressed decoratively in each.[23]

The precept may be debatable but there can be no doubt that, in the hands of Oxenham and other school-story writers, belonging to groups like the Hamlet Club – or Camp Fire or Guides or Guildry – was empowering for girls, as demonstrably it was in real life. Writing in the mid-1970s, Cadogan and Craig were deeply sceptical of the value of all-women associations. One of the lies that the dominant culture has pushed most vigorously in the second half of the twentieth century is that fulfilment for women lies only in heterosexual association, that love between and among women can never equal the tie between individual man and his individual woman. This lie, not in evidence in the nineteenth and early twentieth centuries, when women (single and married) were encouraged to live out their social lives chiefly in the company of others of their own sex, has served to constrain and confine them to the home and the love of one person who, given the way most males have been socialised, is rarely endowed with adequate emotional resources to meet their needs. This theory reached its apotheosis in the 1960s with the (hetero)sexual revolution and declined somewhat thereafter, largely thanks to feminism, which taught us to value women's qualities while submitting men's to rigorous analysis.

The English Folk Dance Society

In adulthood, the Abbey girls' continuing loyalty to the Hamlet Club overlaps with their discovery of a real-life organisation devoted to folk dancing, the English Folk Dance Society (EFDS). Through books dating from the 1920s, the EFDS was to provide the grown-up Abbey girls with an adult version of the 'purposeful association with others' that the Hamlet Club had offered them as schoolgirls. The middle-class discovery of the English country-dance tradition, kept alive by villagers all over Britain, was the result of Cecil Sharp's seeing a team of morris dancers at Headington, Oxford, on Boxing Day 1899. He founded the EFDS in 1911 (the English Folk Song Society had been set up in 1898).[24] Both dances and songs featured in the vacation schools and in Oxenham's depiction of them.

It is difficult today to appreciate how great was the impact of the English folk-dancing movement on girls and women in the first half of this century. Rediscovered in a patriotic, imperialist climate, and following the indigenous revival set in train by William Morris and the Arts and Crafts movement, English folk songs and dances had a tremendous influence on the artistic life and culture not only of the British Isles but throughout the Empire – even I was taught English folk dancing in my Australian primary school in the 1950s. There are many reasons why it was taken up particularly by women. Women had the leisure; the arts and dancing were seen as feminine; women were the teachers of children and the passers-on of traditions.

Dancing was, moreover, an activity which offered women the opportunity to meet with other women in a socially acceptable pastime which kept them fit and was, above all, fun.

Women's health had become an issue when both the Boer War and the First World War revealed the extent of young men's unfitness for armed service: public concern touched women not for their own sake, but as mothers of the race. However, women activists took a more personal view and, recognising the state's indifference and neglect, focused their community work on women's own health needs, and on self-development. The ideals of the Women's League of Health and Beauty, founded by Mary Bagot Stack in 1930, closely paralleled Elsie Oxenham's perception of what the folk-dancing movement offered:

> If Energy is the course of life, and if we women want – as we all do – Life, *we must have energy*. How? – a League – a League of Women who will renew their energy in themselves and for themselves day by day.[25] (Stack's emphasis)

Like organised games in schools, the activities of both organisations were valued by girls and women because they offered freedom from the physical confinement of Victorian and Edwardian young ladyhood: loose clothing, healthy exercise and, above all, social contact. While retaining the outward trappings of acceptable femininity (music, graceful movement and pretty dresses), they were nevertheless empowering. As we have seen, the Abbey girls used dancing as a way of claiming men's territory (dancing on the cloister garth), and in some books teams enjoyed success and achievement in competitions. In addition, the collection and learning of folk traditions and the pursuit of authenticity lent to folk dancing an intellectual and educational aspect as well as a spiritual one: the sense of getting in touch with one's heritage.

The EFDS was not a women's organisation and folk dancing was never intended to be a single-sex occupation. Yet in practice it came close to it. And this was in spite of the fact that most of the characteristic English folk dances like morris and swords belonged, historically, to men. A reader perusing Douglas Kennedy's book *English Dances* (1949) would be struck by the fact that all the illustrations are of men and only one includes women dancers as well. Cecil Sharp's earliest demonstration teams were mainly composed of men. But many of his dancers perished in the First World War, along with so many other British men, turning folk dancing into a hobby largely enjoyed by women and girls. There were simply not enough men left to partner the thousands of eager female dancers, let alone to form teams of their own. And middle-class women had generally more leisure and fewer other social outlets than the men of their class who remained.

Girls' and women's organisations were in their heyday between the wars. Their leaders latched on to country dancing as physically and morally healthy for youth and prospective motherhood. Sharp's early focus on the need to teach young people about their folk heritage put the teaching of country dancing in the hands of educators, who were mostly women. So when Elsie Oxenham became involved with the EFDS in 1920, it was already an organisation whose membership was predominantly feminine. The Abbey books make much of the feminine community which she (and her Abbey girls) experienced in its ranks. Here, for example, we are invited to view the EFDS's Christmas vacation school in the gymnasium of the Chelsea Polytechnic:

The whole six hundred students were gathered there, all excited, all happy, all looking for friends or greeting them eagerly. ...Girls hung over the edge of the gallery to wave to friends just discovered below; girls on the window-sills called greetings to others who had climbed up on the ladders and bars of the gymnastic apparatus; girls ran about looking for chairs or song-books.[26]

(By 'girls' Oxenham meant women, of course. As she mused in another book, 'What were all these girls? Teachers? Students from colleges? They were all grown up, in spite of their short skirts; Jen was the only girl whose hair still hung in plaits...'[27])

And here is Cicely at the summer vacation school in Cheltenham:

for the first time she saw the whole school together and began to sense its atmosphere, of eagerness and excitement, of friendship and good fellowship, of keen artistic joy in beautiful sights and sounds.... The majority of the students were girls, though there were many men...

Oxenham was not interested in the men, but she tells us more about the women:

many of the girls had brilliant jumpers over their tunics and looked more boy-like than ever, with almost no skirt at all showing – especially those who had bobbed their hair, and there were many of them. Keenly interested in everything and everybody, Cicely wondered again how many of these girls were teachers; how many had come because they had found in this folk-dancing the widening and uplift of which Miss Newcastle had spoken; and if it would be possible to make friends outside their own immediate circle.[28]

After the First World War it was evident that many of those associated with the EFDS deplored the takeover of folk dancing by women and children. From the start there was a dispute over whether women should even be allowed to do morris dancing, and this anxiety was reflected in both the EFDS literature and the Abbey books, doubtless because women were constantly aware that they were trespassing on men's privileges which might one day be withdrawn. As Florence Golding wrote in the very first edition of the *English Folk-Dance Society's Journal* (1914):

> The Morris dance is a man's dance and a ceremonial dance, and the flick of a woman's skirt only intensifies that indefinable something in her temperament which always robs the Morris of its predominant feature, viz., the portrayal of strong emotions under absolute control with manly vigour and easy dignity.[29]

Golding here avoids stating what the real concern about women's morris was – that men might have been sexually titillated by the sight of women dancing vigorously, especially in an era when female ankles were only just beginning to appear in public. It was *this* which robbed morris of its 'dignity' when women danced it. The question of women's morris was decided in the affirmative after the war, for the simple reason that 'at the time, women were available and men were not'.[30]

All this explains the significance Oxenham attached to the strength and beauty of the Abbey girls' capers and kick-jumps. She claimed folk dancing – morris and swords as well as country – by the simple expedient of including women within the word 'folk'. As Jen tells Mary:

> 'It's "folk" because it grew among the common people and was kept alive by them; it was never made, any more than a folk-song is made. It's for everybody, not just a few trained and beautiful dancers; anyone can do a country-dance.'[31]

It explains, too, the extraordinary affection the grown-up Abbey girls have for their gym tunics, which gave them a new degree of freedom in the dancing class and the privacy of their home, but which were not considered appropriate for wearing in public, because they revealed too much.

When Sharp died in 1924 his role as Director of the Society was assumed by Douglas Kennedy. Kennedy's crusade during the 36 years of his tenure was to raise the status of folk dancing by trying to divorce it from its associations with the Women's Institute, Girl Guides and schoolchildren – in other words, its association with women. This campaign intensified in the 1930s, which may have contributed to the declining interest of both Elsie Oxenham and Elinor Brent-Dyer in its activities, though Oxenham at least remained a paid-up member. It reached its nadir in 1944, the year Kennedy introduced the American Square Dance to the English public. At his Saturday dances at the Society's headquarters, Cecil Sharp House in Regent's Park, he insisted that only mixed couples should take the floor: 'At first there was a rather large army of unpartnered girls who hoped my heart would soften. But it never did, and soon there was no need.'[32] Because the surplus 'girls' stopped coming, one wonders?

By the time Kennedy came to write his second account of *English Folk Dancing* in 1964, the tenor of the age fully supported his heterosexist policy. He wrote in the preface:

> In spite of the Society's labours to demonstrate otherwise, folk dancing in England is still regarded as right for women and children but not for men. Yet many of the best dances are men's dances, and for the last twenty years I have, through the medium of the Society, presented the social folk dance as one for men dancing with women.[33]

While his concern to include men is quite natural in the circumstances, it is a far cry from the world described by Elsie Oxenham in her accounts of EFDS schools and meetings in the 1920s.

Oxenham reflects the spirit of her times as well as the perspective of a relatively older woman (she was 40 when she joined the Society[34]) encountering the fellowship of the folk-dance movement in its infancy. In *The Abbey Girls Go Back to School* (1922) Cicely finds out that 'there's a society in London ... I'd never imagined grown people, London people, cared for our dances like that'.[35] In the company of several of the Abbey girls she attends the EFDS's summer vacation school, where they meet real-life officers of the Society, easily identified despite the nicknames Oxenham bestows on them: Madam (Helen Kennedy North) and her brother (Douglas Kennedy), the Pixie (D. C. Daking, who really did bring folk dancing to the armed forces during the First World War), the Prophet (Cecil Sharp himself) and the Prophet's Little Page (Sharp's assistant, later his biographer, Maud Karpeles). Cicely and the Abbey girls live out the Society's controversies – dances incorrectly danced, whether women should do morris or swords; and its discoveries – the mummers' play from Yorkshire, the running set from the Appalachians. They also enter into its philosophy: that dancing should be more than educational, but fun, a celebration. They take in the Society's regulations and structure, try for certificates, admire those who have achieved bronze stars and demonstration dresses, subscribe to the journal, buy recordings of the music. After the summer school is over they go to EFDS classes in London. In *The Abbey Girls in Town* (1925) they have a week at the Christmas vacation school in Chelsea, sampling the privations of student accommodation while the keen new friends they have introduced to dancing, Mary and Biddy Devine, are inducted into the community spirit of the Society.[36]

Though men come into these stories – Joan, for example, meets her future husband at Cheltenham – the main emphasis is on the way the movement brought together large numbers of women and on the sense of sisterhood engendered in the almost wholly women-centred world of these interwar years.

It would not be Oxenham writing if we did not find mingled with this sense of community the inevitable element of *noblesse oblige* and of the spiritual beneficence of the folk tradition. Miss Newcastle offers the Abbey girls a description of her evening students and the significance of her work with them:

> 'They're in offices and shops, or else they're little servant-girls from the country with nowhere to go in the evenings, or typists, or cashiers; or girls still at school. I try to give them with – no, through! – their folk-dance work a wider outlet and an uplift they seem to feel the need of, and a touch of music and poetry and art, and I believe they realise it unconsciously; anyway, they respond tremendously and they do improve.'[37]

However patronising this might be in class terms, one does have a sense that Oxenham is partly talking about her own reaction to the dancing. In *The New Abbey Girls* (1923) she has Jen suggest that 'to heaps of these girls, who work really hard all day, in one way or another, these evening classes once a week must be something to live for, something they'll count up the days for, a kind of oasis in a desert'.[38]

Anyone who has attended evening classes will recognise the truth of Oxenham's words; that many people come to classes not simply to learn but to meet people with similar interests. For Oxenham the actual form of the social contact was important; she laid great emphasis on how much better folk-dancing classes were than more sedentary, less inspiring pursuits, like going to the pictures. Indeed, she endows folk dancing with almost mystical health-giving properties, both physical and mental. In *The Abbey Girls Play Up* (1930) Jen explains how folk dancing changed the life of Mary Devine:

> 'I found Mary-Dorothy when she was a typist, starving her imagination in rooms in London. I made her dance, and Joy – my sister-in-law – took her away to the country when the may was out, and we let her wander in Joan's romantic

ruined Abbey. Something – the dancing, or the may-blossom, or the Abbey – touched up Mary-Dorothy's sleeping imagination, and her books are the result.'

'Or the friendship, and the knowledge that somebody had faith in her,' Joan suggests.

Jen denies it. 'She says it was the country-dancing.'[39]

After 1925 the EFDS recedes from Oxenham's books. There has been speculation as to whether there was a falling-out between the author and the EFDS officers she portrayed perhaps too lovingly, or whether the diminished interest was a product of, on the one hand, the author's move to Worthing in 1922, which made it harder for her to keep up with London events (though she founded a Worthing club in 1924 and taught and organised dancing in the district for years[40]) or, on the other hand, her characters' marriages, which led them to focus on more domestic concerns. In the significantly titled *The Abbey Girls at Home* (1929), Joy, now widowed and the mother of young twins, refers to dancing as 'a play thing' and Jen, now pregnant, remarks that dancing no longer comes 'first of everything' for her.[41] With the growing up of the second generation, however, folk dancing once more assumes importance at the Abbey, and the link with the EFDS is restored when Jansy and Littlejan turn to Cecil Sharp House for guidance and are sent Mrs Thistleton – our old friend Tazy from the Swiss books – to teach new dances to the Hamlet Club.[42]

Elinor M. Brent-Dyer and the folk ideal

Precisely as Elsie Oxenham was losing interest, Elinor Brent-Dyer caught the folk bug. In the summer of 1926 she took herself off with a friend, Marjorie Jewell, to an EFDS vacation school where, Miss Jewell told her biographer decades later,

'Elinor was so completely swept away with all the new people, and so absorbed by the whole Folk Dance set-up', that she ignored her companion thereafter.[43]

Dancing then became 'one of her great crazes' and the following year she signed up for a folk-dancing class.[44] It was through the Jewells that she came to meet Elsie Oxenham, when the latter came over from Worthing to Fareham, where they lived, to coach a team of girl dancers including Marjorie. 'This incident shows Miss Oxenham in a pleasant light,' observes Helen McClelland; 'and the impression that she was a genuinely kind person is strengthened by her friendly treatment of Elinor.'[45] For Brent-Dyer, then, the community of folk dancers brought her entrée into the community of writers for girls. Oxenham was then an established writer, at the top of the girls' league; Brent-Dyer still an unknown beginner. Oxenham took an interest in the younger woman's burgeoning career, initiating a friendship which continued until Oxenham's death.

Brent-Dyer was already an Oxenham fan, as we know from *The Maids of La Rochelle* (1924), where '[Pauline] waved one of Miss Oxenham's entrancing school stories as she spoke. "It's lovely! All about country dancing!"'[46] Evidence of the strength of their friendship appears in the dedication to *Seven Scamps* (1927): 'To Elsie Jeanette Oxenham, whose friendship and books have given me so much pleasure, and to whom I owe so much'. A more fulsome tribute appeared in *Carnation of the Upper Fourth* (1934), where Madge lends Carnation some Guide stories and an Abbey book, explaining:

'They will tell you all about folk-dancing. If you're going to be a Guide, you must know about that. Those are a jolly series, too. I always feel as though Joy, and Joan, and Jen, and Mary, and all the rest were real people.'[47]

Here again, it is the community spirit which is emphasised,

linking folk dancing, Guides and the community of the Abbey girls, and reflecting the camaraderie of women writers who supported one another by means of complimentary cross-references to each other's books.

In *Heather Leaves School* (1929), Heather's Christmas present list significantly includes 'any school-stories I haven't got, by Miss Oxenham'.[48]

In Brent-Dyer's later school stories, folk dancing diminishes in importance, becoming merely a school activity which occupies girls with healthy exercise when it is too cold or wet to go out. However, the recently discovered *Jean of Storms* (1930) throws new light on Brent-Dyer's association with the EFDS and demonstrates just how seriously she took folk dancing for a time. *Jean of Storms*, apparently Brent-Dyer's sole excursion into the adult novel, was serialised in the *Shields Daily Gazette* in 1930 and reprinted in book form in 1996. Ostensibly the story of Jean's romance with the local doctor, this is really a book about Jean's friendship with Mollie, her efforts to bring up her two orphaned nieces, and, above all, about dancing. Mollie is a folk-dancing teacher and organiser, and Jean is one of her most dedicated students in a class consisting mainly of women, but including the men they later marry. Sufficient detail is given to indicate that Mollie's class was of an advanced standard and that Brent-Dyer really knew quite a lot about the subject.[49] It is sad, then, that the books she wrote after 1930 lacked the sense of excitement and authenticity which, in *Jean of Storms*, approached that of Elsie Oxenham's novels. From 1930 onwards, it was the school community (and its associated Old Girls' network) which wholly absorbed Brent-Dyer's attention.

From woman to girl: the chain of influence

After the Second World War, the only all-female community which could safely live on in the pages of children's fiction was the girls' boarding school, and its days were numbered. (Even Guide stories were on the way out, and the new career stories, mentioned in Chapter 5, had men strategically placed on the fringes of the plot.) Advocates of co-education had long argued that the single-sex school provided inadequate preparation for living in a heterosexual world, and school stories came to be criticised for the same reason. Critics observed that, in portraying an all-female society, they failed to reflect the reality of social existence, and taught readers nothing about the real world of men and women. Instead of helping to socialise young women for their future roles, it was argued, school stories failed to provide them with the necessary tools, while training them in skills and leadership which marriage and motherhood would render irrelevant.[50]

It was true that there was a conflict between the goals of marriage and motherhood (with, it was implied, social subordination to men) and the education girls received in both the school story and real life. As Cadogan and Craig put it:

> The girls in these books usually are enclosed within an exclusively female society: characterization, if nothing else, demanded that qualities which had been regarded as 'masculine' should be allowed to occur in certain girls – usually the principal characters. These act on their own initiative, are concerned with forging their own position in society, are shown to be capable of leadership, aggression, inventiveness, intellectual effort. But the implications of this are rarely followed up: where a definite conclusion has to be drawn to a girl's activities, the sentimental equation of marriages with 'happy endings' has proved irresistible ...[51]

As we have seen, however, many authors did try to bridge the conflict by presenting unusual marriages and even unmarried adult heroines. And what Cadogan and Craig overlook is the fact that the very qualities inculcated in girls' schools and school stories – not simply 'leadership, aggression, inventiveness, intellectual effort', but also cooperation, friendship, supportiveness and service – were encouraged and fostered in associations of girls and women and in informal circles of women such as the groups of young mothers portrayed by Elsie Oxenham in the Abbey books of the 1930s and by Elinor Brent-Dyer in *Jo to the Rescue* (1945). The skills and qualities developed in the girls' schools and girls' organisations fitted them excellently for participation in adult women's groups like the Women's Institutes or folk-dancing clubs and, in particular, for leadership of girls in schools, Guides or other such associations.

For single women in particular – and remember that there were more single women in Britain in 1921 than ever before in recorded history – the path from girls' to women's world was clearly signposted. As we saw in Chapter 3, single women were encouraged to 'sublimate' their 'maternal instincts' in community work with girls. All three of our authors accepted this role – a role which combined social approval with the possibility of leadership and which recognised achievement – in their teaching and girls' clubs and, of course, in their writing. In her Abbey books Oxenham offers us a fictional representation of the spinster in this situation in a minor character called The Writing Person. Described as an older woman who took up dancing quite recently and who writes books for girls, including Camp Fire stories, she is, of course, Elsie Oxenham herself in a cameo role.[52] The Writing Person claims to find in folk dancing an inspiration for her work, and points out that the same is true of 'nearly all' the women at the EFDS evening class:

> 'If you talk to them for long, you find they have "girls" in the background. ... Sometimes it's children in their day-school classes; most of them are teachers, of course. But very often it's big girls, Guides, or a club, or Guildry, girls to whom they're teaching folk-dancing in the evenings, mostly just for the love of it.'[53]

Miss Newcastle, another EFDS contact based on a real person, is one such woman. By day she teaches small children:

> 'But at night I teach folk-dancing and songs and drill to all kinds of girls – girls' clubs, Y.W.C.A. girls, ex-munition girls, a big gym class on Mondays, and so on. I look forward all day to the evenings, though I enjoy my work and I'm very fond of my kiddies. But I'm keener on my big girls, and they simply live for their classes.'[54]

As we gasp at her energy – how many of us would teach every day in a school, every evening in adult education? – we also recognise precisely how the woman-centred perspective was passed on, no doubt to Douglas Kennedy's irritation.

In *A World of Girls* I suggested that country dancing was for Oxenham a kind of metaphor for women's friendships.[55] Certainly for her the two ideas were inextricably linked. If we view it thus then we can see the Hamlet Club and the EFDS on a continuum, with the one a preparation for the other. In other words, if Elsie Oxenham's schoolgirls were being socialised for living in the adult community, it was a community of women that was envisaged and into which they slipped naturally and inevitably.

These were the women who went to dancing classes and vacation schools and ran clubs for girls, as Miss Newcastle had described. The Camp Fire handbooks emphasised that the role of Guardian was ideal both for mothers and for

> younger women who are lonely and wish for whole hearted companionship, for women who wish for someone to 'mother,' for women who wish to increase their power of service to the community.[56]

Thus society validated women's leadership of other women and girls by reframing it in terms appropriate to femininity –

motherliness and service – and as a cure for the 'loneliness' inevitably associated with spinsterhood. However, when school-story writers depict it in their books they give quite a different impression, and theirs, I would argue, is the correct one.

Women taking control

All the big movements for girls set up in the early years of the twentieth century were explicitly intended to prepare girls for their traditional feminine roles as servants of men and the community, and as carriers on of a healthy race (the language of eugenics was prominent at this time). However, all of them actually succeeded in transmitting quite different messages, which were much more liberating and women-centred.

Girls' Guildry, which features prominently in Bruce's Maudsley books, was founded in 1900 by a Glasgow man, Dr W. F. Somerville, with the express goal of teaching girls 'to become Christian women' and to develop 'qualities of womanly helpfulness'.[57] Bruce was associated with the organisation for over 30 years, rising to become the Centre President of the West London branch in the 1930s.[58] The Girl Guides were founded in 1909 to train suitable wives and mothers for 'the future manhood of the country'.[59] Guides are important in the first half of the Chalet series, and Brent-Dyer's biographer suggests that the author, like her heroine Madge, may have attended a Guiders' course at the Guide training centre at Foxleas in the New Forest. Certainly she was active in Guiding in her Hereford days.[60] Oxenham also wrote many books about the Guides, but her preferred girls' organisation was Camp Fire – on the face of it the most conventional of all. American in origin, dating from 1912, it had similar goals, activities, rewards and structures to the others and clothed them in a manufactured aura of romance, heavily influenced by native American culture, and cynically designed to lure the girls in.[61]

And yet in all three movements, girls and young women had opportunities previously undreamt of: physical exercise, teamwork and independent action, exemplified by the popular activity of camping, as well as the acquisition of a variety of useful skills, many of which were not normally associated with femininity in those days. They learned initiative and female solidarity, to strive for their own sakes and to put themselves (and their sex) first: not at all the message that Lord Baden Powell and Dr Somerville had in mind. Even Camp Fire, with its emphasis on femininity and its long fringed gowns and beads and candles, can be reframed in positive ways. That Oxenham was aware of the justifiable criticisms of the movement is evident from several of her novels where Camp Fire and Guides are set in rivalry and their respective merits and drawbacks debated.[62] But it is plain she would rather have the gentle 'womanliness' of Camp Fire, with its unregimented ways and feminine accoutrements, than the quasi-military, pseudo-masculine vigour of the Guides. This refusal to emulate men simply because they are leaders, and to learn useful skills simply because women should be useful, can be interpreted as quite radically feminist, even as it almost certainly spelt the death-knell for the movement: for only those things which mirror masculine institutions can be valued in a patriarchal society, and what is 'different' will almost always be viewed as inferior.[63]

What happened with girls' organisations, in short, was the not unfamiliar phenomenon of women taking control of movements intended to ensure their own subordination, and using them for their own ends. Their male supporters probably never envisaged the degree of confidence girls would gain from success in new tasks and from access to rewards, uniforms, rituals and activities like camping, hitherto available only to boys. Though often dismissed in the later part of the twentieth century as 'proto-fascist',[64] these organisations with their esoteric trappings allowed girls to lay claim to their own space, symbols and ceremonies, and helped to diminish what had long been seen as 'natural' differences between boys and girls in terms of abilities and interests.

But possibly their most radical contribution came in the opportunities they provided for women to assume leadership roles and to become role models for younger women. Girls' organisations dominate a large proportion of school stories before the Second World War, including many of the novels of Elsie Oxenham, Dorita Fairlie Bruce and Elinor M. Brent-Dyer. Of the three, Bruce has not come into this chapter much but she, like Oxenham but much more than Brent-Dyer, focused on leadership and service (admittedly with a class bias which jars today). It is perfectly clear that she did not see participation in Girls' Guildry as a useful training for marriage and motherhood: in *Dimsie Intervenes* (1937), bossy Erica Innes sets up a branch of Girls' Guildry as preparation for her intended career as an MP![65]

5 Careers

School-story heroines, with few exceptions, were middle class; and the provision of career opportunities for middle-class girls had been one of the main campaigns of Victorian feminists, leading to the opening up of many professions hitherto closed to women. The impecunious Victorian spinster had to become a governess or a lady's companion, neither occupation secure, well paid, or even particularly pleasant. For a woman to have to earn her own living was, frankly, a misfortune. But the rise in the numbers of unmarried women, who could not look to husbands for support, coincided with the expansion of British industry and commerce, creating openings for such women in shops and offices; education was made compulsory in 1880 for children up to the age of ten, and reformed at all levels, leading to a demand for school teachers; nursing was professionalised; medicine and, in 1919, law were forced to admit women to their ranks. Higher education was opened to women after 1869. Still few people associated the word 'careers' with the word 'women'.[1] Even the examples of women like Elizabeth Garrett, who fought to become a doctor even though there was plenty of family money, and who went on working after her marriage,[2] and Florence Nightingale, who preferred to organise a profession than to live off her fortune or a husband,[3] failed to challenge the notion that personal fulfilment was no ground for the pursuit of paid work by a woman. By the turn of the century feminists were writing of professional life as an *alternative* to marriage for middle-class women or as a useful *preparation* for it, but these ideas were slow to gain acceptance within the dominant ideology, where marriage continued to be seen as the only desirable goal, and career and marriage as mutually exclusive. There are any number of autobiographical accounts from the late nineteenth and early twentieth centuries of women's struggles to break free from a purely domestic existence, and contemporary novels reflect these debates.[4]

In 1868 the Taunton Commission had exposed the shortcomings of Victorian middle-class girls' education. Those girls lucky enough to attend the new-style academic girls' schools founded or reformed after that date – institutions like Miss Buss' North London Collegiate and Camden Schools, Miss Beale's Cheltenham Ladies' College, the Girls' Public Day School Trust schools, and the girls' public schools like St Leonard's, Wycombe Abbey and Roedean – were offered an education which would fit them for a career, should they want one. For Margaret Fletcher, a student at Oxford High School in the 1870s, there was already a strong expectation that girls would go on to work:

> It had been explained to us that we must all look forward to doing something for ourselves. Girls must have some sort of career.[5]

Indeed, the need for girls to prepare for employment was one of the main justifications for the feminist campaigns to improve girls' education in the late nineteenth century. Increasing numbers of middle-class fathers were finding it impossible to support their adult daughters at their leisure, and those women thrust untrained on to the employment market had a thin time of it. Besides, if professions like medicine were to be open to women, girls needed a sound academic background; and the same was true for the traditionally feminine, but now reformed and organised, occupations like nursing and teaching. After the First World War, reported Sara Burstall, headmistress of Manchester High School, even well-to-do parents began to see the desirability for their girls to earn a living.[6]

Nevertheless, the idea that women worked if they needed the money, and did not work if they didn't, persisted well into the interwar years, as is evident from the novels of all three of our authors. The Second World War marked a watershed; after that we rarely see this philosophy again, apart from one or two obviously anachronistic instances, such as Bruce's novel *The Serendipity Shop* (1947), where the tale centres on Merran Lendrum's difficulties in finding a job because she has not been brought up in the expectation of having to work and has had no training for a career. 'Daddy and Mummy, bless their hearts, hoped they might keep you at home till you married.'[7] This is really the plot of a Victorian novel – Gissing's *The Odd Women* (1893) makes a good parallel, since it too depicts a doctor's daughters left to fend for themselves after his unexpected death – but it is 50 years too late.

After the Second World War it was taken for granted that girls' schooling would prepare them for work – at least until marriage. Josephine Elder's novel for girls *Exile for Annis* (1938) expresses this new ideology. When Kitty declares that she plans to marry and have twenty children, Annis responds: 'That's not a thing you *be* . . . You've got to be something before that, a teacher or a secretary like your mother was.'[8] The idea of girls having a career (rather than simply an occupation) *instead* of marrying, or one which persisted beyond marriage and motherhood, was still unusual – but not, as we shall see, unknown.

Leading useful lives

'Forty years ago we divided ourselves into two classes,' Winifred Peck explained in her autobiography of 1952, *A Little Learning*: 'those who meant to earn their living, and those whom we described, not always aptly, I fear, as Home Sunbeams'.[9] Oxenham's early novels neatly illustrate this division. The wealthy Abbey girls, as we saw in Chapter 1, did not need to work. But Cecily Perowne, apparently parentless, had to be trained to earn a living. Joy and Maidlin may pursue their musical vocations but Cecily, equally talented, 'must be a dressmaker, or a clerk, or a cook, or a shorthand-typist; in her spare time she can be a musician...'[10]

Yet even conservative writers like Elsie Oxenham recognised that some women wanted to work, even when they did not have to. This was particularly the case for unmarried women, who had no homes, children or husbands to care for, but the desire became almost a duty for Oxenham's wealthier heroines, who found themselves in an analogous position to spinsters since servants performed most of their domestic labour. Oxenham's novels from the first three decades of the twentieth century focus on the necessity for such women to lead *useful* lives, however 'idle' they might be in economic terms. She places the responsibility on the shoulders of the women themselves:

> 'Phil and I ... see the difficulty for girls who can't take paid posts because they don't need them. But I'm certain there are things for everybody to do; we only have to find our own job.'[11]

For such women, unpaid philanthropic employment was the age-old remedy. So well-to-do Fran from the Gregory's books hopes she will be allowed to go to college: 'I should think we could go without having to pass exams, and take certificates, unless we really wanted to', and then take up some form of (unpaid) 'social service'. But her twin, Phil, has other plans for when she leaves school:

> 'Have a good time – go out a lot with mother; travel; play tennis and golf well enough to get into the finals of

tournaments, in the jolliest clubs I can find to join; go to dances in the winter and take up amateur theatricals; and, of course, go on with my music, and sing and play really well.'[12]

At school Phil cannot understand why Fran seeks out Suzanne, 'who'll probably be a teacher in an elementary school in a few years', rather than Marjory, who 'comes from that huge house with the lovely gardens up beyond the station'.[13] Fran is motivated by a combination of *noblesse oblige* and a wish for useful occupation which gives her a greater sense of fellow-feeling with Suzanne, preparing for a career, than with leisured Marjory.

The heroine of this very class-conscious novel has to leave school and get a job because her mother needs expensive medical treatment. Like so many school-story heroines, she becomes school secretary at her old school, but worries lest her former schoolmates should cease to be friendly towards her now she is 'in business'.[14]

While never questioning the notion that rich girls should not take jobs from those who need them, Oxenham leaves us in no doubt that her sympathies lie with Fran and Ven, and repeatedly indicates that employment makes young women more mature. When we next meet Phil and Fran, their schooldays behind them, they seem naïve and unworldly by comparison with Ven, who 'had a decisive business-like air, which their sheltered lives had not given them. "I'm a working woman, my children!" Ven would say . . .'[15]

Several novels turn on the problems which arise when wealthy heroines do not find useful outlet for their energies. In *The Troubles of Tazy* (1926), for example, Tazy, who has been a forceful schoolgirl and popular leader in two earlier novels, finds herself without role or purpose when her schooldays come to an end. Trapped in the small British community of the alpine village in Switzerland where her mother must live for her health, she loses all the qualities which made her a moral champion at school:

> 'She's the best of good souls, and good company, and great fun; but you can't depend on her. It's a pity, for with her energy she could do so much. As it is, it's no use trusting her. ...Tazy has too much time on her hands. ...She's clever, and full of energy, and she has nothing to do. ...I don't think she ought to be allowed to live here just wasting her time in little nothings.'[16]

Her English visitors, Fran and Ven, think she ought to get involved in community work. Fran tells Tazy that she

> 'ought to be mixed up in big jolly movements, working with keen people who do things because they believe in them. You can organise and run things. ...You don't need a paid job; you mustn't take one, of course, for it would keep out some girl who needs it. But there are societies who can't afford to pay. ...You ought to be organising secretary in some big settlement or institute... You'd get on well with people.'[17]

Sadly, the solution Oxenham produces at the end of the novel is a husband. The reader feels cheated, not simply because this is so clearly a cop-out, but because we haven't even had the fun of a romance leading up to Tazy's capitulation. Two chums from her schooldays appear out of nowhere, and there seems no particular reason why she accepts one rather than the other. Her friend Karen warns perceptively that 'she'll still be Tazy, and brilliant and full of energy, even after she's married. She may not find herself busy enough, and in that case she'll still need an interest in big things, or she'll be as restless and undependable as ever.'[18] Oxenham duly brought Tazy back (married and with two little girls) into the Abbey series much later, as an English Folk Dance Society teacher and organiser – which, as we saw in the previous chapter, was for Oxenham exactly the sort of 'big thing' Karen described.[19]

Dorita Fairlie Bruce's books share many of Oxenham's attitudes to careers. In her interwar novels, for example, she accepts that women from families with money might not seek paid employment, and that girls like Coral Danesbury (in *Dimsie Goes Back*, 1927) and Tibbie Macfie (in the Springdale books) might have 'social careers ahead of them' and 'need to train themselves for the sort of life they're going to lead'.[20] Interestingly, in Bruce's novels such characters tend to derive their wealth from fathers who have made fortunes in industry, not, as with Oxenham's, from membership of some great landed (and probably titled) family.

Before the Second World War Brent-Dyer, too, had plenty of characters who 'won't do anything after they leave school but help their mothers and play tennis, and go to dances,' as Madge says of Birdie Woolcot and Gwen Jones in *Carnation of the Upper Fourth* (1934).[21] Even as late as 1952, Anthea Barnett and Elma Conroy, students at the Chalet finishing school, are described as 'people who needn't work.'[22]

But even 'society maidens' have obligations to society and to themselves, and are expected by Bruce to substitute for paid work a regime of community service and self-education. As Miss Yorke, headmistress of the Jane Willard Foundation, observes:

'It isn't in the nature of things that you can all have professional careers, but no one need develop into a mere butterfly, and very few of the Jane Willard girls have done so, thank goodness! Look at Rosamund Garth! A society damsel to the finger-tips, with a slate full of gaieties, yet she finds time for her Guildry work and art lectures.'[23]

Sheila Ray's suggestion that *Wild Goose Quest* was actually written long before its publication in 1945 is supported by the way its heroine, Katharine, continues to occupy herself with unpaid 'do-gooding': as Ray notes, 'There is no question of Katharine looking for a real, paid job, despite the reduced circumstances of the Raesides'.[24]

Perhaps most significantly, school-story writers did not see marriage as bringing a woman's obligation to the community to an end. Jen, for example, has persistent qualms about the 'futility' of her life as lady of the manor, wife and mother:

> 'There are such big things to be done in the world, and here am I opening bazaars and giving away prizes and taking the chair at the Women's Institute! It seems so footling.'

Her friends point out that her work is important nevertheless: 'Lots of the fêtes are for hospitals,' they say soothingly.[25]

A suitable job for a woman: women's work up to the Second World War

Many of Oxenham's heroines start out as secretaries; it was work with which she was familiar, having acted as her father's secretary before her own writing career took off and freed her to type nobody's work but her own. From her very first book she preferred to situate her secretaries in a domestic setting, displaying a repugnance for office life which is startling in its forcefulness. In *The Junior Captain* (1923), Christine, whose father has died, has to leave school and 'train for office-work. I hate the idea.'[26] In *The New Abbey Girls*, published in the same year, Joy says she would 'die' if she had to work in an office,[27] and Jen repeats the sentiment no fewer than three times in its sequel, *The Abbey Girls Again* (1924).[28] Mary Devine, about whose situation she is commenting, clearly has no attachment to her job, probably because a typist's life really was unrewarding, the hours were long and the work dull and poorly paid.

> Mary's earnings [supplied] just enough to make a home possible, with very little to spare for extras ... [B]oth she and Biddy [her fifteen-year-old sister] were looking forward to the day when Biddy would be earning, too, though from different motives. Mary hoped for some relief from the grind and strain of the last few years; Biddy had visions of a good time, when she had money of her own to spend.[29]

Biddy is studying at a London commercial college 'to prepare herself for a similar post'.[30] Oxenham rescues both Mary and Biddy from the typing pool, though not from typing: Mary becomes Joy's secretary, and Biddy is despatched to a French firm through a Hamlet Club contact. In *Maidlin to the Rescue* (1934), Rachel and Damaris, too, are rescued – this time from a tea-shop – because 'they're too good to be wasted serving in a shop, or typing in an office'.[31] Fortunately there is always room for another assistant to the Abbey girls: 'Rosamund is going to want help at the Rose and Squirrel as soon as Audrey marries; and Maid needs a secretary.'[32]

Other early books focus on the conflict, real enough to many real women, between pursuing one's personal career goal and being a good daughter-at-home. Patience is training to be a missionary. But her grandmother, who brought her up, becomes ill, and she feels she must give up her studies to care for her. 'You could afford a nurse, couldn't you?' 'Afford six! But we're not going to have one.'[33] At the end of this depressing tale, Patience herself is rescued by her cousin Sally, who comes to take her place, freeing Patience to return to college. Sally is providentially a 'born nurse' but, luckier still, her mother has just died and 'She has no home now and nothing to do.'[34] Poor Sally!

With so many heiresses, Oxenham does not dwell too much

on careers – more on jobs and vocations. She offers us dancers and musicians, gardeners, tea-shop and tuck-shop pro-prietresses, cooks, children's nurses, teachers and, of course, writers. Many of them work for one Abbey girl or another. Ann Rowney comes to the Abbey as a journalist, fills in as temporary cook, and ends up running Jen's rest home in Yorkshire.[35] None of these jobs is a standard nine-to-five post and many are self-employed. All are traditional feminine occupations except perhaps that of the gardeners, who certainly raise a few eyebrows, mainly because of the picturesque smocks and breeches they wear. Finally, they are all creative: that this was important to Oxenham would explain her abhorrence of office life.

Dorita Fairlie Bruce lays more emphasis on careers than Oxenham. 'Jane's is a jolly fine school,' Dimsie declares in *Dimsie Moves Up Again* (1922).

> 'You can tell it by the older girls, if in no other way. They're all doing something to be proud of. Joyce Lamond got her degree at Girton last term'... 'And Hilda Heathley had a miniature in last year's Academy...'[36]

In point of fact, Cambridge did not officially grant degrees to women until 1948[37] – the last British university to do so by a long way – but Bruce persists in sending her characters there: 'Old Eric [Erica Innes] seems to be having a glorious time at Cambridge.'[38] In adult life Dimsie recognises how the girls' aspirations were considered and catered for in the school curriculum. She acknowledges their debt to Miss Yorke:

> 'Why, we always told you everything – how Jean was to be a poet and Mabs a journalist, and Erica meant to get into Parliament. And you fitted it all into our school-work – gave Jean special composition, and Mabs précis-writing, and encouraged Erica to get up the debating society.'[39]

In general, these youthful dreams come true. Mabs does become a journalist – 'The sub-editor [of *Home Fires*] says he has never met anybody with such a natural gift for collecting news'[40] – and Jean a poet, as absorbed in her art in adulthood as in the days when she neglected her duties as Head Girl and was deposed.[41] Erica, however, becomes only the secretary of an MP, and then his daughter-in-law – not an MP herself. Pamela, alternately destined for a sporting career and for exploration, achieves neither, to her friends' disappointment; luckily, a husband comes along, and she becomes (rather unexpectedly) the first of the Anti–Soppists to marry.[42]

Careers are given even greater prominence in the retrospective Dimsie school story, *Dimsie Intervenes*, published a decade after its predecessors, reflecting the changes in social attitudes by that time. Dimsie's chosen career – medicine – comes at us out of the blue, and is equally promptly snatched away, when her father's death removes the resources necessary for the expensive training. Bruce re-used this plot device in a novel of 1956, *Sally Scatterbrain*, in which Jane Woodroffe is forced to leave school because her family can afford to educate only one daughter, and her clever sister wants to be a doctor.[43] What worked in 1924 is less realistic in 1956, when scholarships or excellent free schooling and grants for university would have been available to talented students.

Dimsie makes the most of her disappointment, turning her energies to cultivating the 300-year-old herb garden at her family home in Scotland and selling the produce to drug companies. Here, though her first encounters with the masculine world of Glasgow business are not happy ones, Bruce cannily makes a successful commercial enterprise out of what is essentially a feminine tradition. The herb garden at Twinkle Tap was originally cultivated by Dimsie's ancestress, the Grey Lady, who 'narrowly escaped drowning as a witch' – a reputation which Dimsie is warned may attach to her, too: 'People will call you a female quack...'.[44] Fortunately for Dimsie, while most doctors are deeply sceptical about alternative medicine, Peter Gilmour shares his wife-to-be's belief in the efficacy of herbal remedies, and suggests that she 'found a woman's school of medicine, and train up a generation of disciples to follow in your steps. Then you may be acknowledged years hence as a great and wise physician.'[45] (Dimsie, of course, disclaims any interest in fame.) In the event, however, they marry, and work together in an unusual partnership dispensing both herbal and conventional remedies to their joint patients.

Dimsie's profession is one of those described by Mary Cadogan and Patricia Craig as 'just on the right side of orthodoxy'[46] and by Eva Löfgren as one of a 'slightly eccentric choice of careers among Bruce's heroines'.[47] But it is unorthodox and eccentric only to modern patriarchal eyes: what really characterises this and many other options Bruce puts forward is that they belong to a world of women. Löfgren mentions Bijah Allen's plan to write biographies and Sally's wish to do animal portraiture. These are both careers in which women had been successful. Certainly Bruce, like Oxenham, preferred to give her girls creative jobs. A novelist is fortunately able to endow her heroines with the requisite talent to pursue careers in, for example, music (Nancy Caird, an organist; Ursula Grey, a cellist); writing (Sylvia Drummond, a novelist; Jean Gordon, a poet), and art. Desdemona Blackett is destined to become a great actress but, luckily, has artistic gifts as well, enabling her to secure a post as designer in a textile factory during the war. This serves the interests of the plot of *Nancy Calls the Tune* – Nancy would hardly have seen much of Desda if she had been touring in ENSA like her sister Celia, for example – but it also demonstrates how Bruce adjusted her principles in wartime to allow her characters to take commercial positions as employees since normally, like Oxenham, she favoured self-employment. Thus, during the war Toby Barrett and Charity Sheringham, two of Bruce's best-developed characters, farm, as do two other Blackett girls, and Jill Ewing goes as gardener on a big estate, freeing a man for war service.[48]

Teaching

One of the most acceptable careers for women in the period leading up to the Second World War was teaching. It seemed a natural extension of the nurturing role expected of women and, if confined to girls' schools, offered no threat to the male status quo. Through their teachers (always called 'mistresses' in the books), the girls of the school–story series were provided with role models of respectable leadership and successful career women. Teaching was also an occupation close to many writers' hearts: a surprising number were teachers themselves, and wrote with first-hand knowledge of the profession and empathy for its practitioners. Elsie Oxenham was not among them, and it shows: her schoolmistresses are stiff, unsympathetic characters, inclined to stand on their dignity, and plainly not of the same social class as her heroines. It is true that the Abbey girls maintain an easy relationship with their former headmistress, Miss Macey, but Joy's disrespectful references to 'Mackums' suggest that she never comes to see the older woman as either mentor or friend.

Where they *are* of equal social status, you can be sure that some unusual circumstance has caused them to take up paid employment. In one early novel, *The School Torment* (1920), it is made clear that Dorothy Grant did not *need* to work: 'it was not absolutely necessary'; she had a small income from her father, and 'would always be welcome' in the homes of relatives.[49] But Dorothy is keen to ensure that the little sister for whom she is responsible gets a good education, having done brilliantly in Maths at Newnham herself. Thus the pair end up at a boys' school in Wales with Dorothy teaching – all the masters have 'joined up' in the First World War – and her sister as pupil. Plainly the story-line of a girl at a boys' school appealed to Oxenham (who used it more than once: see *At School with the Roundheads*), but equally clearly, she needed an excuse for Dorothy to embark on a career. More common in Oxenham's books is the situation of the young woman who planned to teach but who 'comes into money' and gives up the idea. Joan Shirley, for example, meant to teach games and drill; she would, states Jen, 'have made a splendid schoolmistress if she hadn't inherited the Abbey'.[50]

Bruce is more positive about teaching as a career than Oxenham. Lesley Musgrave, Diana Stewart and Jill Ewing all become teachers and her headmistresses, in particular, are both more idealised (in terms of wisdom) and more human; they establish friendships with their colleagues, prefer certain girls to others, and are allowed the occasional headache or moment of indecision. If temporary heads or house-mistresses take a wrong-headed approach to their work, their mistakes and inadequacies can be measured against the excellence of the permanent staff. The girls speak of their teachers with affection; Oxenham's of theirs (when they speak of them at all, which is rare) with apathy.

Quite different from both is Elinor Brent-Dyer's approach. It is hardly surprising to find that there is a strong tradition in the Chalet books of former students returning to teach at the school. Teaching was Brent-Dyer's own profession and, in literary terms, there could be few better ways to bring favourite characters back into a school story. Juliet Carrick, Grizel Cochrane, Gillian Linton, Mary and Peggy Burnett, Biddy O'Ryan, Nancy Wilmot – the list is not exhaustive – all come back at some point to teach. Several subsequently marry and leave; but those who choose sanitarium doctors for their husbands (quite a crowd, including Hilary Burn, Biddy O'Ryan and Grizel Cochrane) contrive, like Jo, to remain within the Chalet ambit even after marriage. Pam Slater, on the other hand, leaves the Chalet School precisely because she wants to move on in her career: 'I've been here ten years and I feel I'm getting into a rut.' Aiming for a headmistress-ship, she wants to try out a few theories of her own, and 'I don't fancy they'd be acceptable here.'[51] Nancy Wilmot, who replaces her, is a rare career woman, dedicated to a life of teaching. Kathie Robertson, too, who runs the Kindergarten on the Görnetz Platz – she who assured us in *The Chalet School and the Island* that she could never teach: 'I shouldn't have the patience!'[52] – also seems set to stay. Len Maynard, of course, also plans to teach; and many fans foresee her eventually taking over from Nancy Wilmot as headmistress of the school.

Spanning nearly half a century in production, the Chalet series depicts the increasing professionalisation of teaching across the twentieth century. Madge Bettany is not deterred from setting up a school of her own by the fact that she has no background in education; her colleague, Mademoiselle Lepattre, has been a governess. Very soon, though, a university degree is expected; Miss Wilson has been at the London School of Economics, Juliet Carrick read Maths at Royal Holloway. Even the games mistresses are Bedford-trained, and the wartime gardening mistress has studied at Swanley. *The New Mistress at the Chalet School* (1957) follows the progress of Kathie Ferrars, just down from Oxford, in her first teaching post. Like most of her colleagues, she has had no teacher training as such and has to learn on the job. All Chalet mistresses are good at what they do but some, like Kathie Ferrars and Nancy Wilmot, are particularly popular with the girls because they have a real flair for the work. Brent-Dyer makes the point that all the degrees and experience in the world will not make up for an absence of talent or a lack of interest in girls: the locum headmistress in *Gay from China at the Chalet School* (1944), Miss Bubb, is a case in point.

Where Brent-Dyer really scores is in her depiction of the warm, supportive community of women teachers, which has the feel of a substitute family. She makes a job at the Chalet

School sound like heaven on earth or, as Kathie Ferrars puts it, 'The dream of my life!'[53] The cosy staff-room scenes after hours, reading, playing games, drinking coffee and sharing gossip about students and vacation plans, banish any ideas the reader might have entertained that life on the isolated Görnetz Platz – shut up in a chalet with two dozen women and 200 girls and nowhere to go and nothing to do in the rare off-duty minute – might actually be claustrophobic and boring. Because so many of the staff remain at the Chalet School across large parts of the series, unlike the girls, who grow up and leave, some of the mistresses become her most popular and enduring characters. It is in Brent-Dyer's staff room, in fact, that the world of women is at its most appealing.

Work and marriage

When Madge Bettany announces her forthcoming marriage in a book of 1927, it is taken for granted that she will give up work after the wedding.

'But won't she teach in the school any more? Why, it won't *be* the Chalet School without Madame!'...

'With a house to look after?' Joey spoke in her most sarcastic tones. 'Don't be silly!'[54]

The idea that women should relinquish paid employment upon marriage persisted for much longer than the idea that women with means of their own should not work. Indeed, in many occupations between the wars (including local authority teaching) an official or unofficial 'marriage bar' operated, leading some women teachers to conceal their wedded state so as not to lose their jobs. Again, the justification was that married women did not need the money because they were supported by their husbands (whether or not this was in fact the case), whereas men had families to support (at least in theory) and single women had to support themselves. Even in the postwar years, personal fulfilment for women was still perceived as belonging to the private domain, arriving without question with marriage and motherhood.

This attitude was typical of the girls' school story, but there were exceptions. Biddy O'Ryan (Courvoisier) stays on as history mistress at the Chalet School for one term after her marriage, until the school can find a suitable replacement, but then leaves, her impending motherhood already evident.[55] Jo Maynard fills in briefly after an accident temporarily removes four mistresses. She leaves her baby in the staff room while she teaches, but in a dispute with the locum headmistress makes it clear that her first duty is to the child. 'I'm his mother, and it's my real job.'[56] Widowhood may bring women back into paid employment. Frau Mieders is a long-term Chalet mistress, Mrs Redmond (the former Miss Durrant) returns briefly.[57]

In Dorita Fairlie Bruce's novels, the loss of so many apparent career women in marriage has disappointed many readers. Eva Löfgren comments:

> To Erica, prefectship and head girlship is a training for a possible political career in the same way as it is for a boy prefect and future colonial officer. But ... she will end up, not in Downing Street but in a Scottish manor house, restricting her energies to the Red Cross and local charities.[58]

It is true that Erica suggests, 'I may still be an M.P. even if I do marry Derrick. It isn't impossible, you know.'[59] But Dimsie thinks it inadvisable and in the 1920s she was probably right. Certainly in *Dimsie Carries On* (1946) there is no sign that Erica – now mother of a young family – retains her dream of political life.

But Bruce also gives us an unexpectedly high proportion of career women who do not disappear in marriage: both those who do not marry – including Mabs Hunter, Jean Gordon, Sylvia Drummond and Tony Semple in the Dimsie books alone – and those who marry, but continue their work, like Dimsie herself. Sarah Burn has observed that both Oxenham and Bruce leave their writers unmarried, an interesting and possibly self-referential comment.[60] But Elinor Brent-Dyer, coming that much later when spinsterhood was more of a bogey, gives *her* heroine, Jo, the whole lot: a family which would kill most mothers, and unparalleled literary success.

Many of Oxenham's major characters, too, have a particular talent, like Joy's composing and Maidlin's singing, whose exercise can be combined with marriage and motherhood, particularly when one has servants and nurses. She draws the line at ballet – Damaris must give up dancing to marry[61] – but Lisabel comes back as gardening mistress when her husband is away, bringing her baby daughter with her.[62]

What is clear is that Oxenham's eyes were opened up in the 1920s by the lives of the new friends she made in the English Folk Dance Society. *They* did not give up work on marriage:

> 'Do you suppose Madam could settle down in her tiny flat, beautiful as it is, and enjoy it, after teaching folk-dancing all these years? She's too full of the love of it; she must go on teaching, and making new people love it too, and go about giving it to fresh people.'[63]

This was quite a radical view for 1923; and though Oxenham did not adopt it for many of her heroines, the idea resurfaced with surprising vigour in one of her last books, *Tomboys at the Abbey* (1957).

In this retrospective title, Gudrun is torn between a career as an actress and her love for Karl, a sailor, who wants her to marry him and settle down. Gudrun is reluctant to give up the stage. Joy says: 'And I suppose Karl isn't willing to give up the sea and stay at home, if you marry him?' Gudrun is sure he would never do that.

'It's not fair,' proclaims Joy. 'You're to give up your career and settle down to keep his house, while he goes to sea and leaves you at home and only comes back to you between his voyages. Why should you do all the giving-up?' Joan, more moderate, wonders, 'Has anybody suggested that you should marry Karl and still be an actress?'

'Lots of actresses are married,' Joy agrees.

'He wants to come first,' says Gudrun.

'But he isn't willing to put you first,' Joy points out. '... It ought to be the same for the man as for the girl.'[64]

This 1950s Joy is clearly a different person from the 1920s Joy of the same age. Oxenham has brought her heroines' views bang up to date, though she carefully balances Joy's more extreme judgements with Joan's restatement of more traditional values:

> 'Of course, if you decided to go in for having a family, you'd need to give up the stage for a time. But you could go back later on. Having a family must be the very happiest thing in the world – worth even giving up the stage for.'[65]

Jobs for women after the war

In 1947 an article appeared in Elinor Brent-Dyer's *Chalet Book for Girls* entitled 'What do you want to be – and why?' The date of its publication is significant. By 1947 Brent-Dyer was writing full-time and needed to be able to turn her hand to a range of literary genres – not simply the short stories which had filled the pages of interwar annuals for girls to the exclusion of any 'serious' or non-fiction items, but also the factual or advisory pieces now considered an essential part of postwar publications. (Hence her essays 'Cooking in Olden

Times' and 'Beauty for the Teen-agers' in the same volume.)
Critics were calling for greater 'realism' in writing for young
people. Finally, postwar Britain was caught up in discussion
and debate over the part that women were to play in the
society of the future. Was it to be the traditional domestic role,
as desired by many citizens longing for a return to 'normal
family life' after the wartime upheavals? Or was it to include
greater participation in the paid workforce, as required by the
economy and fought for by feminists?[66] Brent-Dyer's opening
lines set the scene:

> Not such a very long ago, there were two occupations for
> girls: to be married or to become a governess. ... Today,
> practically every profession and trade is open...[67]

In these lines she also, of course, laid her cards on the table.
Elinor Brent-Dyer was not very interested in restricting
women to a domestic career and, in fact, never mentioned
marriage again in the four-page essay. Unmarried herself, and
not much of a homemaker – her *Chalet Girls' Cook Book* is
testimony to this! – she had worked all her life and, while
marrying off most of her fictional heroines in accordance with
the dominant ideology, had been careful to provide them all
with an education which prepared them for a career. It is true
that the continental girls mostly left school only to prepare for
marriage and that, before the war, some of the English girls did
not contemplate taking up paid work or further training (Jo
being the most obvious example). However, the interwar years
had seen a steady increase not only in the work available to
middle-class women but in the expectation that many would
have to work to support themselves.

We can only guess how Brent-Dyer welcomed the changed
attitudes of the postwar years when paid work became the
norm. But the fact that she included an article on careers for
girls in her *Chalet Book for Girls* was almost certainly a response

to social pressure rather than simply a personal crusade. It is no coincidence that advice on one career or another is given in practically every girls' annual of the 1940s and 1950s. The future role of postwar women was of major concern not only to educators but to politicians and social commentators of every sort, anxious to determine the shape of tomorrow's Britain. The impetus for this came from two sources. On the one hand, there was the economic imperative. Britain needed wives and mothers, yes, but it also needed skilled workers. With the introduction of free secondary schooling for all in the 1944 Education Act, the old idea that careers were only for boys was scotched for ever. By 1947 Brent-Dyer would have assumed that very few of her readers would now leave school to face, as Jo did, neither job nor further training. On the other hand, as we have seen, marriage and motherhood still tended to bring an end to a woman's working life, and most wives anticipated never having to enter the paid workforce again. It was well known that many girls went into any old job after leaving school, confident that they would be rescued by a husband sooner or later; and that this expectation also deterred some parents from supporting their daughters through a full education or training for a career. Desertion and divorce – still uncommon, but increasing – or the death or illness of a husband might cause such women to revise their plans; and it was these women, as well as those who might not marry, that the social commentators were concerned to influence.

There was, in addition, a strongly held conviction that it was unfeminine for a girl to enter certain professions, or to aim high in any. The pursuit of wealth, earned by oneself rather than by one's husband, was not an issue in these pre-Equal Pay days. So how could Brent-Dyer sell the idea of a career, when many girls saw paid work only as a brief interlude between school and married life?

She did it by talking about personal fulfilment, an idea largely absent from pre-war discourses:

Making money is not the most important thing in life, although it is necessary that everyone should be able to be self-supporting if, or when, the need arises. To be happy in your employment is much more satisfactory.[68]

There was nothing here about the needs of society or the priority of marriage and motherhood. For Brent-Dyer, as for Oxenham and Bruce, the feelings of the woman were paramount: her happiness, her enjoyment of her job. And no reader of Brent-Dyer's fiction would doubt for a moment that she was sincere in asserting the importance for girls – indeed it was their right – to fulfilment through work.

Careers advice in the postwar years differed from publication to publication, but Brent-Dyer's suggestions for girls were among the most idiosyncratic. In the *Chalet Book for Girls* article her artist chose to illustrate, with one exception, only the obviously feminine jobs: respectively, receptionist; commercial artist; dancing teacher; piano teacher; milliner; stablehand; nurse (though Brent-Dyer actually mentions nursing only in passing); and schoolteacher. The exception is a picture of what might be a woman architect, a career Brent-Dyer *does* refer to; she is depicted at the drawing board, with ruler, set-square and compasses to hand.

The article sets an aggressive tone from the start. These days the suggestion that a girl might consider working in a bank might be thought unadventurous in the extreme, but in 1947 Brent-Dyer was challenging a strongly held association of men with numeracy and money when she observed: 'There is, I believe, no reason, apart from the convention that banking is a "man's job," why women should not become bankers.' She pointed out that during the war many banks had women tellers, 'and jolly good they were'. She next claims the male bastions of medicine and law: 'Women are, of course, freely admitted now as doctors and solicitors.'[69] 'Freely' was a bit of an overstatement, given the quotas and discrimination that have limited women's participation in these professions even up to the present day; but, assuming she was aware of the situation, this kind of persuader language might be read as an attempt to counter that very prejudice. It is true that her radical light is momentarily dimmed by the unfortunate aside that 'conveyancing work seems to be suited to girls'. (This reasoning, which I have seen repeated in much more recent writing on legal careers, doubtless because conveyancing is associated with 'the home', reserves the most routine, lowest-paid and lowest-status work for women, leaving the more glamorous and remunerative areas of legal practice for men.)

But this is nothing to Brent-Dyer's next suggested career for girls, which is – of all things – the church! She mentions the famous Congregational preacher Maude Royden in an approving tone which reads oddly coming from someone brought up as a member of the Church of England (where female priests were not to be admitted till almost half a century later) who converted to Roman Catholicism (where female priests are still out of the question).

After this she becomes a little more conventional. There is advertising: 'girls are advised to start out as typists or secretaries and work your way into the more important jobs later'. Commercial art is followed by the more interesting suggestion, 'Architecture could do with a few women – if only to plan sensible kitchens that can be worked easily.'[70] After chiropody comes cooking (at this point she seems to be working through an alphabetical list). Then there are teaching, farming, hotel work, dressmaking and veterinary work. This last is not a surprising choice for an animal-lover like Brent-Dyer but it is interesting that she aims so high – veterinary science is second only to medicine in its competitive status – rather than suggest that girls become kennelmaids or, as the illustration shows, stablehands. Dancing instruction and 'mannequin-work' complete an eccentric list. Brent-Dyer has apparently not caught up with the vogue for air hostesses, and there are no newspaper reporters here either.

Even when she recommends a traditionally feminine sphere of work she manages to challenge conventional notions of women's role. She tells of a milliner of her acquaintance

> who has made a marvellous success of renovating hats and teaching millinery in night school. ... Her business, which is run in her flat, does rather show that the most successful girls [*sic*] are those who, trained in the groundwork of their chosen calling, branch out in some original aspect of it, or build their own special kinds of businesses.[71]

It's a useful piece of advice. Women *can* succeed in their own enterprises, but only if they are careful not to compete with men and to find their own distinctive niche.

Wider horizons

The postwar concern with women's work was reflected not simply in articles on careers for girls but also in a new literary genre: the career novel. For 30 years such novels (*Air Hostess Ann, Social Work for Jill, Rosemary Turns to Teaching* and the like) played a significant role in children's publishing, and then disappeared more or less without a trace. They left their stamp, however, on school-story writers, many of whom tried to move into the career-story market as school stories became increasingly unfashionable.

Dorita Fairlie Bruce was one of them. For a time she abandoned the school story to concentrate, in the four modern Colmskirk novels, on work for women. As Sheila Ray observes:

> The world was changing and a new type of book, the career novel for girls, was emerging; these were written for

schoolgirls and were about young women earning their living, pursuing careers and, usually in the end, getting their man as well.[72]

Bruce plainly believed that useful occupation was as important for women as for men: the unfairness of their grandparents' marriage settlement, which provided 'liberally' for the boys' education but not for Lalage and Susan, is foregrounded in *The Debatable Mound* (1953).[73] But she tended to stick to the creative, self-employed types of career she had always preferred for girls: the kinds of jobs which gave them plenty of control over how they spent their time. So she continued to indulge her passion for the land and growing things (she shared Oxenham's love of gardening), offering us Jane in forestry[74] and Susan in fruit farming.[75]

In Chapter 1 we noted how Merran Lendrum protected the independence of her little shop – and herself – from the threat of takeover by big businessman Sam Bartle. Yet Bruce allows her sister Julia, who knew even at school that she wanted not to marry but 'to train as a super-secretary', to become Sam Bartle's personal assistant, in which position she can temper his capitalist enthusiasms and direct his philanthropic energies.[76] Julia, like Erica, has political ambitions; unlike Erica, she is not yet married off, though Bruce keeps Sandy Lamond waiting in the wings. In this postwar book (1947), Julia is a much more modern depiction than Bruce's earlier secretaries, Winifred Arrowsmith and Dimsie Maitland, who both return to their old schools as secretaries,[77] and Nell Connor, who goes as secretary to Bruce's other Grey Lady, Marcia Johnston, the author.[78] Yet the personal nexus which characterises these appointments is still there; in Nell's case, even in the Second World War, it virtually amounts to charity. Only in the very late title, *The Bartle Bequest* (1955), does a heroine (Primula Mary Beton) obtain her post in open competition; so it is particularly sad that, as we saw in Chapter 2, she makes a disaster of it. Moreover, it is not a particularly accurate depiction: a

171

contributor to *Serendipity*, Doreen Litchfield, castigates Bruce for providing Primula with a housekeeper, a luxury her curator's salary could not have sustained in the 1950s. 'I have noticed that those who have never worked, i.e. been in paid employment, have little idea what it means to live on a salary,' she comments, adding that Bruce was probably reflecting her own circumstances here, as 'she was never without domestic help of some sort'.[79]

Given Brent-Dyer's propensity for taking up new ideas, and her willingness to try out a range of literary styles, it comes as something of a surprise to find that the career novel appears not to have appealed to her. Someone who in the early 1950s could turn her hand to formats as diverse as geographical readers and mixed-sex adventure tales should surely have been able to polish off a career novel with ease. But the only work of hers which could be said to fall into this category is *Kennelmaid Nan* (1954), which gives a reasonable picture of the qualifications and qualities required of a kennelmaid and the duties she performs, but has a mystery element as well. In this it differs from the very practical career novels of the Bodley Head or Chatto & Windus series, but resembles the much more glamorous *Ann Thorne, Reporter*[80] sort of book: the adventure story set within the context of a particular calling.

However, in her postwar novels, written contemporaneously with the career-story vogue, Brent-Dyer clearly demonstrates the influence of the genre. That careers for her characters were of genuine interest to her is shown by the amount of attention she gives to the subject in what are first and foremost school stories. Chalet girls have serious discussions about their future work among themselves and with their elders (good examples take place in *The Chalet School Goes to It,* 1941, and *The Chalet School and the Island,* 1950) and long sections, even whole chapters, are devoted to updating readers on their progress once they have left school (see *Changes for the Chalet School,* 1953). Naturally, the occasional engagement is also announced, sometimes bringing professional hopes and dreams to an abrupt end, but the tone is completely different from that of Elsie Oxenham, whose updates tend to consist of a series of birth announcements.

Brent-Dyer's approach to careers for girls in the *Chalet Book for Girls* article combined the received wisdom of her era with some quite radical notions. By and large, this is true of her fictional girls too. Her heroines aim high. Elinor Pennell plans to be a *top-class* secretary, and even Joan Baker hopes for more than the typing pool. When Bride Bettany is thinking of a career as a librarian (she changes her mind later), she wants a post at the Bodleian or the British Museum.[81] The gardeners, popular with Brent-Dyer as with Oxenham and Bruce, envisage their career as a business, not a hobby.

Nursing as a career is understandably popular with Chalet girls, but so is medicine. At least four girls – Dorothy Brentham, Vicky McNab, Daisy Venables and Margot Maynard – are destined to be doctors. Julie Lucy trains for the Bar. Now there are 50 career novels about nursing to every one about medicine for women – indeed, I am aware of only one twentieth-century British girls' career novel about medicine, Joan Llewelyn Owens' *Margaret Becomes a Doctor* (1957) – and none (in Britain, at least) about women entering the legal profession, so Brent-Dyer is advanced for her time here. Many Chalet girls – for instance, Joan Sandys – go into scientific careers. Mary-Lou's decision to become an archaeologist also represents a challenge to tradition, as does Eustacia Benson's fame as a classicist.

Aside from the usual musicians (Margia, Gay, Jacynth, Nina) and artists (Clem, Vi, Sybil with her art needlework), perhaps the most obviously feminine role of which Brent-Dyer approves is the religious life. Luigia, Mary, Robin and Margot all become nuns, and Tom is an urban missionary. Although ballet is mentioned (Felicity Maynard) and horse-riding (Norah Fitzgerald), neither of these popular career-novel options is taken very seriously.

By far the largest number of career novels concern nurses

(the Sue Barton and Cherry Ames books; *Jean Becomes a Nurse* and its sequels). Air hostesses and journalists come next. The fashion industry was also a big draw, broadly encompassing careers ranging from sales assistant to buyer and manager, from model to designer. These were fields in which women were certainly visible at this time – according to the census of 1961, 90 per cent of nurses, 20 per cent of journalists and 12.5 per cent of sales personnel were women – but, unlike Oxenham's and Bruce's worlds of women, they were often at the service of men, assisting male doctors and male flight crews, or caught up in industries which objectified women for men's delectation. In real life, over a quarter of all working women were secretaries and typists and, in the professions overall, women comprised only one in ten, the proportions ranging from 59 per cent of teachers and 48 per cent of social workers to 3.5 per cent of lawyers and 2.3 per cent of engineers.[82] Teachers and social workers feature in the girls' career-story lists, lawyers and engineers only (of course) on the boys'.

Clearly, then, Brent-Dyer's ideas about possible careers for girls were much more ambitious than those of the 'official' career novels, not to speak of the reality for most women. School stories have traditionally been criticised as conservative, but it is plain that in the ideas they conveyed about women's work, outside marriage or within it, they challenged many current ideologies. Small wonder that girls preferred to read the works of school-story writers to the career novels for girls, and that the school-story series have lasted whereas the career novel has all but disappeared.

Changing perspectives

Oxenham's work is almost completely untouched by social or literary movements to encourage careers for girls. In this she is far and away the most old-fashioned of the three writers. She gives her heroines scope to be creative in their work, and argues in favour of a useful life of service rather than dilettantism or the pursuit of financial reward. But then she cushions her heroines from the disempowering consequences of what she advocates by endowing most of them with private incomes and permitting the rest to become beneficiaries of the heiresses' good fortune.

Yet it is clear that Oxenham admired women who worked for a living and manoeuvred to give them pleasant environments and conditions of work, shunning the masculine workplace (symbolised by the 'office' and 'business life') in favour of self-employment or a personal arrangement. All her working heroines continue to occupy the world of women, whether it be the school, the tea-shop, the dancing class, or a friend's nursery, kitchen or garden. There are few battles to be fought with patriarchy here, and women can get on with their lives unimpeded.

Bruce's world of work is characterised by a feminine value system as strong as Oxenham's. This is shown by the judgement of Maudsley headmistress Miss Hale, that Nancy Caird's artistry will take her far, but 'the human factor will always enter largely into Nancy's calculations, which will make her a woman first and a musician afterwards'.[83] This was the kind of heroine Dorita Fairlie Bruce liked.

Brent-Dyer was much more in touch with career movements for women than Oxenham or Bruce. The circumstances of her life – born just that much later and just that much poorer – meant she had to take paid employment, and in a job which kept her abreast of modern trends. This enabled her to assimilate, rather than reject, the idea that young women must be prepared not simply to work but to enter careers which had once been men's preserves. She did not entirely dispense with the personal contact – most of Jo's mother's helps are old Chalet girls – but professional training now went hand in hand with word of mouth. Though many

Chalet mistresses are Old Girls, Kathie Ferrars gets her job in open competition on the strength of an Oxford degree and linguistic facility.[84]

Brent-Dyer retained enough of the old separate spheres heritage in her world-view, however, to reject the glamour professions and service industries promoted by so many of the new career novelists. This was partly class bias, of course: Mary Evans has suggested that the academic curriculum of girls' schools at this time was only partly intended to open doors to good jobs:

> That determination was undoubtedly there, but so too was the determination ... that middle-class girls should remain in the middle-class world. The surest way to do this was, in the 1950s and 1960s, to go to university or training college or medical school or some other enclave of middle-class expectations or aspirations.[85]

But it was partly because, like Oxenham and Bruce, she was attached to the world of women. Many of Brent-Dyer's characters end up back at the Chalet School, and it serves as a refuge even for former career women like Eustacia Benson.

While Oxenham and Bruce gave women power in their separate worlds, and career-story authors endeavoured to create resourceful, independent heroines in conventional, often oppressive, work situations, Brent-Dyer aimed to widen girls' horizons. Her late school-story heroines, like Mary-Lou and the Maynard triplets, bring us full circle: they are 'young and free' role models for the 1960s, not free in the sense their mothers were, with time on their hands and money in their pockets, but free to choose from a broad range of career options. With increased choice, of course, came increased hazards. These young women had to move out of the world of women and fight for space on the patriarchal stage.

By killing off Mary-Lou's parents the author explicitly freed her to follow in her father's footsteps. But the triplets, tied by their family links as well as by their career choices (teacher, writer, nun) to the world of women, seem destined to come back to it.

Conclusion

This book has argued that the novels of school-story writers Elsie Oxenham, Dorita Fairlie Bruce and Elinor Brent-Dyer depict what can be described as 'a world of women'. The books are significant historical documents which sometimes mirror changes in society's perceptions of women's roles, goals and relationships (as, for example, with their increasing concern with careers) and sometimes challenge the dominant ideology. The time-scale for *A World of Women* roughly coincides with that chosen by Joseph McAleer in his *Popular Reading and Publishing in Britain 1914–1950* (1992), in his case because it represents 'the first time the mass reading public was commercially managed and exploited in a recognizably modern way'.[1] McAleer includes a chapter on Mills & Boon romances in his survey and also one on children's literature, which is, however, predictably disappointing on girls' school stories. The statistics testify to their popularity (they were far and away the most enjoyed books among East Ham schoolgirls in a 1932 survey)[2] but McAleer's discussion is confined, as so often, to Angela Brazil.

Throughout this period, with the exception of the war years, the dominant image of British woman was domestic, and the new mass-market women's magazines like *Good Housekeeping* (founded in 1924) and *Woman* (1937) concentrated on heterosexual romance, housework and childcare to the almost total exclusion of positive alternative interests.[3] With the school-story series, on the other hand, though practically all heroines fall in love, marry, have children and keep house, these are far from their sole or even major preoccupations (partly, of course, because they had servants, which most *Good Housekeeping* and *Woman* readers did not), and school-story writers included many single and career women among their approved characters. The greatest contrast lies in the narrow focus of the women's magazines, directing women's gaze inward into the nuclear family in the home, and the wide focus of the girls' school stories, looking outward towards friends, jobs, and community activities with other women and girls.

Flourishing between the Victorian/Edwardian world of separate spheres and the sexual revolution of the 1960s, girls' school stories perpetuated ideas of sexual segregation that were becoming increasingly unfashionable throughout this period, especially towards the end. They were able to do this because the genre was essentially a conservative one, produced for a conservative market, and because the ideas were ones with which their authors had grown up and which seemed right to them. In so doing they resisted the full force of the pressure exerted by critics, who from the mid-1930s pressed for children's literature to be more 'realistic' – which meant, *inter alia*, to give greater prominence to males and mixed-sex activities and which culminated in what can be termed the heterosexualisation of children's literature in the 1960s. By then, luckily for them, our three authors had come, or were coming, to the end of their writing careers. For with heterosexualisation came the destruction of the traditional girls' school story and its replacement by mixed-sex adventure, family and career stories and, eventually, teenage romances. Simultaneously, the advent of television in the 1950s and the commercially inspired introduction of a new kind of magazine intended for teenage girls combined to transform the adolescent world-view from girl-centred to a focus best described in the title of one of the magazines, *Boyfriend*.[4]

Even in the first half of the twentieth century, authors could not entirely resist social trends. Oxenham, Bruce and Brent-Dyer all made adjustments in an effort, albeit half-hearted, to meet the new imperatives. Oxenham, whose early books are characterised by moving portrayals of intense relationships between and among women, shifted in the 1930s towards a 'finding-herself' theme for the growing-up years of her second generation of Abbey girls, Rosamund and Maidlin. In the 1940s she put the spotlight on younger heroines in the Abbey series (both the retrospective and the continuing titles) and concentrated on heterosexual romance in her Rainbows novels and, towards the end of the decade and into the 1950s, the remaining Abbey books. But all these romances continued to take place in a social and emotional world of women.

Brent-Dyer tried her hand at mixed-sex adventure titles in the Fardingales/Chudleigh Hold books of the 1950s and the non-school Chalet titles *Joey and Co. in Tirol* (1960) and *A Future Chalet Girl* (1962). But in her last years she reverted to the tried and true Chalet formula which, fixed in its predictability, kept her going till her death. Bruce's non-historical Colmskirk stories of 1947–55 were charming excursions into the light romance genre: Sheila Ray has suggested that 'as possible teenage fiction, the Colmskirk novels were ahead of their time'.[5] But the late Sally books represent a return to the old-style school story. It was the genre Bruce was clearly happiest with, but it was out of favour with the critics, and from 1961 to her death nine years later she published no more novels. Sheila Ray confesses that she was actually responsible for advising Brockhampton Press to reject a manuscript from Dorita Fairlie Bruce in the mid-1960s: 'it seemed hopelessly out of date'.[6]

Despite their attempts to respond to critical demands, taken as a whole the books of these three authors must be characterised as books for and about women. Not only did they describe a world of women in a literal sense, in that men were largely absent, symbolic or irrelevant, but they also depicted a world in which women's values prevailed. Oxenham, Bruce and Brent-Dyer conceptualised a feminine value system as one which, deriving from the separate spheres philosophy, allocated women responsibility for morality, emotion, cooperation, support, connection and nurturing. These are the dominant values of these novels, much appreciated by fans of both sexes, and they seem to be shared by some of the most approved men in the stories as well as the women. Where men behave in ways which the authors see as typically masculine – and this is most common in the work of Brent-Dyer, who, as the youngest of the three, was probably most influenced by modern notions of appropriate gendered behaviour – their influence is often minimised by feminine mediation.

Yet alongside these traditional feminine values all three writers endowed their heroines with qualities which derived from the ideals of first-wave feminism: independence of thought and action, a strong sense of self-worth, a desire to do something more important than simply marry and reproduce, and the actual ability to succeed, both in these goals and in their marriages and parenthood. All school-story heroines can drive a car, for instance. But all of them have cars to drive. This gives them important physical freedom, and they are further assisted by nurses and governesses who take the children off their hands. School stories naturally recognised the importance of education for women and, later, careers for everyone including the well-to-do, at least until marriage. In the case of heroines like Dimsie and Jo, who worked from home, giving up their career even after marriage was simply not considered. 'I never see you sitting down with a piece of embroidery as Mother used to do,' Jack Maynard teases his wife, who retorts: 'No; and as long as the publishers like my books, you never will, my lad.'" Equal rights in the broadest sense are taken for granted in these novels, and there is never any sense that women are or should think themselves inferior to men. If anything, the opposite message is delivered.

*

One thing is clear: readers appreciate the grown-up characters in girls' school stories. How else can one explain the fact that a good proportion of the space in the fanzines is taken up with critical discussions of adult characters (Miss Annersley, for example) or characters who grow up in the course of the series (Benedicta Bennett, Nancy Caird)? Undoubtedly as readers get older, we become more interested in the adult characters. I well remember as a child reader skipping over the first chapter of *The New Chalet School* (1938), which takes place in the school staff room, because I had little interest in the conversations of adult women; now it is one of my favourite scenes in the entire series.

Certainly when the authors were still alive, readers engaged vigorously with their heroines' fates. Dorita Fairlie Bruce, for example, was repeatedly asked for more Dimsie stories by people who could not bear to let their schoolgirl idol go: she obliged with a retrospective school story (*Dimsie Intervenes*, 1937), a wartime thriller featuring Dimsie as wife and mother (*Dimsie Carries On*, 1946), and several short stories.[8] Where the original authors failed to supply full enough details about their characters, fans have not hesitated to fill the gaps. Meg Crane's continuation of Thekla von Stift's life and her detailed biographical study of Miss Wilson won widespread acclaim from Friends of the Chalet School members.[9] A startling number of fans have written sequels to both Abbey and Chalet sagas, and these are also eagerly read even though they run the risk of treading on other people's dreams. *Visitors for the Chalet School*, Helen McClelland's 'reconstruction' of an infill Chalet story based on notes left by Elinor Brent-Dyer, was published in 1995 and promptly sold out, even though it is really more McClelland than Brent-Dyer (though none the worse for that).

Whatever we think of these unauthorised additions to the canon – and many fans hate them – they offer striking evidence that, on the one hand, people *care* enough about their school-story heroines to want to go on finding out more about their lives and, on the other, they feel they *know* the characters sufficiently well to be able to get inside them and continue their stories in ways which are accepted and even appreciated by other people who know the characters just as well as they do. While writing *Visitors for the Chalet School*, Helen McClelland confessed that she 'found it as easy to write about Elinor's Chalet School people as about my own family and the friends I know really well'.[10]

This also accounts for the tongue-in-cheek continuations which occasionally grace the pages of the more light-hearted journals like *Folly*, whose authors provide futures for their fictional heroines which, one can safely guess, are worlds away from those their original creators would have designed – yet are still in character. Kate Tyler's spoof first chapter of a book entitled *The Abbey Girls Revisited*, which appeared in *Folly* in 1993, is a fair sample:

> 'Brownie, my dear!' Cicely hailed her joyfully from her bathchair in a dark corner of the tithe-barn. 'Congratulations! The first of us to reach a hundred grandchildren!'[11]

A favourite device of sequel writers is to introduce characters to the modern complications of adult life – complications from which their creators kept them mercifully free. So the new generation of Abbey and Chalet characters find themselves, in the fans' continuations, facing adultery, divorce, homosexuality, sterility, broken vows and prison. *Nothing* is sacred.

The many layers of readers' engagement with school-story characters were accurately observed by Joy Wotton in a New Chalet Club *Journal* of 1997:

> Who would doubt that in a literary world, far away, Joey did indeed have her quads? But, why do we care whether Len's

marriage to Reg was a success?... Why don't we read decent literature?

The reason, she suggests, is that:

> Perhaps reading novels and juvenile fiction is not an escape from reality, but a form of process meditation, providing a framework to explore ideas about ourselves and our situation and gain a grasp on reality.[12]

This may explain why so many readers feel the urge to incorporate their favourite school-story characters into the late twentieth-century world with which they themselves must struggle.[13]

Bridget Fowler concluded after interviewing women who enjoyed romance fiction that 'the type of literature women read is linked to their wider world-view'.[14] I would argue further that our choice of reading not only reflects our world-view but helps to mould it.

This is borne out by Shereen Benjamin's article in a *New Chalet Club Journal* of 1998, where she specifically links her youthful reading of girls' school stories to her pleasure in their all-female canvas. For Benjamin, as for myself and countless other readers, the stories bore little resemblance to her own circumstances and she found it hard to make sense of her 'addiction', until:

> Much later I came to see the roots of a resistance in my obsession with girls' school stories; a resistance to a world dominated by the unremarked and taken-for-granted assumption that heterosexual relationships were a normal (indeed, the *only* normal), natural and inevitable part of adult life. The fantasy world of girls' school stories was more than an escape from this incomprehensible world, for it opened up a space where adventure and female friendship

counted for more than my own daily reality of schoolwork and pressure to secure a boyfriend.[15]

Benjamin grew up in the 1970s but, as we saw in the Introduction, already by the 1960s the reading of girls' school stories was so taboo among teenagers (not to speak of adult women) that we generally indulged our secret vice only in conditions of the utmost furtiveness, concealment and shame, usually unaware that hundreds of others shared it.

Since the advent of the appreciation societies and the fanzines (and the web-sites and e-mail chat-lines), all this has changed. Life now imitates art, for at their gatherings the fans, too, occupy a world of women: a world which is largely female, largely adult and largely based on the traditional feminine values of the girls' school stories. As with the school-story heroes, male fans who accept the dominant (female) value system are successfully integrated into these circles. I would not wish to carry the analogy too far since, however optimistically one reads the novels, it is risky being quite so idealistic about real people. But I am sure that most fans like the feminine nature of their societies, in large part because it offers a rare space free from masculine contempt and disapproval, where we can share our love of the books and discuss things that matter to us openly and seriously.

Of course, it is extraordinary that at the end of the twentieth century women still *need* a space where they can cherish their own traditions, away from the patriarchal world's disapproval. The increasing number of male fans of girls' school stories and supportive male friends and partners whom I have met through the appreciation societies encourages me to believe that attitudes may be changing, as do the more respectful tone and the invitations to contribute and explain tendered by mainstream academics, school-story (i.e. *boys'* school-story) enthusiasts, publishers and the media. On the other hand, recent history demonstrates that men continue to be reluctant to share power – newspapers at the time of writing report continuing discrimination in the worlds of golf and cricket, for example – or to acknowledge that women might have a separate, different reality (or set of realities, for we are all different) from the official patriarchal world-view. Hence the extraordinary number of disgraceful sexual harassment cases in the news. Late twentieth-century courts, like late nineteenth-century ones, continue to be occupied with domestic violence, rape, and cases of men killing their female partners (a much more common occurrence than the other way round), suggesting that many men still feel the need to control and punish women. The greater sympathy and leniency which the courts tend to extend to these cases than they do to assaults by women on men indicate that such manifestations of male control of women are neither unexpected nor, apparently, inexcusable. Ridiculing the gentle harmless traditions women love while filling our cultural world with macho sex and violence which degrade and destroy women is an extension of this masculine control and punishment.

A world of peaceful, egalitarian relationships such as those promoted in girls' school stories, where girls and women are allowed and expected to be self-directed and self-fulfilling, seems an impossible dream for the foreseeable future. But the fact that so many of us have striven for these goals and are reasonably happy with our lives in the circumstances is testimony perhaps to the influence of the girls' school-story ideals and role models.

As a teenager in the 1960s, I joined Elinor Brent-Dyer's Chalet Club. The twice-yearly *News Letter* kept me in touch with the still evolving Chalet saga. Every issue was self-evidently written by the author herself and a good proportion of its contents were directed at the hundreds of fans (there were 4000 members at its peak) who wrote to her about the books. To each one Brent-Dyer replied seriously, the choice of language and tone contributing to the impression that the Chalet School was a real place and its characters actual live people.

> All Joey's girls are too young to think of marriage as yet [she wrote in No 15, September 1966]. The Triplets are not yet eighteen and as they all intend to take a university course they have no time to take such thoughts seriously. It is true that Dr. Entwhistle shows an interest in Len, and Len is beginning to have some inkling of this; but whether it will come to anything later on neither I nor anyone else can tell you at the moment. Con has little or no time for anything but her writing; and Margot has far other ideas about her future. ... We must wait to see how things work out for all three.

Even in my extreme youth I never thought the Chalet School was real – young readers quickly grasp the difference between fiction and reality – but I cheerfully joined in the shared illusion, sending off my entries to the competition in each *News Letter* cleverly designed to test market opinion and suggest ideas for future novels. One competition asked us to pretend we were a new pupil at the school writing our first letter home; another to rank a list of titles in order of preference, prizes going to the lists which most closely approximated Brent-Dyer's own view; a third solicited essays about our favourite character. The names of prize-winners and honourable mentions were published in the next *News Letter*, and mine appears more than once. In No 19, the last Brent-Dyer wrote (for No 20 was put together by her publishers after her death), she described me as 'one of our most faithful contributors, Rosemary Auchmuty, of Newcastle, New South Wales'.

As I stare at the words I have a vision of myself as a young woman in 1969 with my future before me, with no particular career or training in mind (except that I was certain I would not teach), a half-formulated desire not to end up like my mother (who was actually a terrific person with a pleasant, fulfilled life) and no strong views on whether or not I would marry and have children. But one thing was clear to me, even then: I would look after myself. I would do what I wanted, as far as my circumstances permitted. I had to earn my living, of course – my generation did – but work would be a means to an end. My primary goal was to follow my dreams.

I have no doubt what put these self-indulgent ideas into my head. If the Abbey, Chalet and Dimsie books did no more for me, they taught me that the lives of girls and women matter, that *my* life mattered, and that my happiness was to be measured in terms of *my* self-satisfaction, not the happiness of my family, my prospective husband or my children, as laid down by so much literature for women, from classics like *Little Women* through my mother's magazines of the 1950s to the sexually explicit novels we were supposed to enjoy in the 1960s. No one told me to train for a useful, safe profession which would secure me a livelihood (let alone the affluence I took for granted from both my parents' lifestyle and the school-story world); I was left to 'find myself'. The result was that I followed my dreams to London, where I scratched a living in part-time jobs for eleven years before embarking on a career in middle age. Quite early on I made a conscious decision not to marry. As for children, I never really wanted them enough to do anything about it.

Thirty years after Brent-Dyer's death, I look at my students (for of course I did end up teaching) and think how different their world is. In many respects they have a much shrewder, better-informed idea of what lies ahead than I had at their age. As the product of the optimistic, liberal 1960s, with my head stuffed full of outdated ideals from girls' school stories, I simply never bothered about the things which concern them most. If I had no particular career in mind, it was partly because Joy and Jen and Jo never thought in terms of career – but also because careers were still not much emphasised for girls in the

1960s. (Of course, like Jo, I wanted to write, but two or three years as a 'professional' writer soon convinced me that a living income from writing can be made only by the rare few.) If I couldn't quite see how motherhood might be fitted into my life, it was partly because the nurses and servants whom Joy and Jen and Jo took for granted were not available to people like me – but also because we still live in a society notoriously unfacilitating to working mothers.

Clearly the school stories were, in these respects, totally inadequate preparation for adult life in my era. How much less useful they must be for today's young women! My students inhabit a cut-throat world of joblessness and homelessness, ambition and competitiveness. They are preparing to enter a racist and misogynist profession (I teach law, but many jobs share these unattractive characteristics). They will face a thousand patriarchal obstacles, as I did, before they reach their goal, if they ever do: try getting through barrister's pupillage without suffering sexual harassment, or having a baby without losing your job in a solicitor's firm. Perhaps, like me, they will be diverted to a side track; perhaps, as I did, they will find this more fulfilling. Women's lives tend not to follow a linear path, though they may be all the more rewarding for this.

Yet in other respects the girls' school stories gave me the soundest of foundations. The aim of Elsie Oxenham, Dorita Fairlie Bruce and Elinor Brent-Dyer in their 'growing-up' books was to inspire girls, to give them confidence to move into a womanhood they deliberately portrayed in an attractive light. Too attractive, perhaps, to be realistic, but it worked for me. I have enjoyed my grown-up years because, inspired by girls' school stories, I have followed my dreams. I don't think I am alone in this.

Notes

Abbreviations

DFB   Dorita Fairlie Bruce
EJO   Elsie Jeanette Oxenham
EMB-D   Elinor M. Brent-Dyer

Full details of works are only given in the Notes where they are not included in the Bibliography.

Acknowledgements

1   Mary Cadogan and Patricia Craig, *You're a Brick, Angela!*, 1976, 2nd ed. 1986. Mary Cadogan, ed., *Chin Up, Chest Out, Jemima!*, 1989; and books on women detectives in fiction, women and children in wartime fiction, flying women, and romances.

2   Sheila Ray, *The Blyton Phenomenon: The Controversy Surrounding the World's Most Successful Children's Writer*, André Deutsch, 1982

3   Helen McClelland, *Behind the Chalet School,* 1981, 2nd ed. 1996. Monica Godfrey, *Elsie Jeanette Oxenham and her Books*, 1979; a longer biography is in preparation.

4   For a review of critiques of girls' school stories, see the Introduction to the Girls' Volume of the forthcoming *Encyclopaedia of School Stories* (Scolar Press), edited by Rosemary Auchmuty, Hilary Clare, Robert Kirkpatrick, Sue Sims and Joy Wotton.

5   See, for example, Margaret Marshall, *An Introduction to the World of Children's Books*, Gower, 2nd ed. 1988, p.157

6   P.W. Musgrave, *From Brown to Bunter: The Life and Death of the School Story*, Routledge & Kegan Paul, 1985; Jeffrey Richards, *Happiest Days: the Public School in English Fiction*, Manchester University Press, 1988; Jeffrey Richards, 'The School Story', in Dennis Butts, ed., *Stories and Society: Children's Literature in its Social Context*, Macmillan, 1992

7   Sheila Ray, 'School Stories' in Peter Hunt, *International Companion Encyclopedia of Children's Literature*, 1996, pp.348–59

8   Rosemary Auchmuty, 'The School Story: From Brazil to Bunty', in Nicholas Tucker, ed., *School Stories: From Bunter to Buckeridge,* National Centre for Research in Children's Literature, 1999

9   See note 4

10   McClelland, 'In Search of Elinor'. In Auchmuty and Gosling, eds., *The Chalet School Revisited*, 1994, p.62

11   Shirley Foster and Judy Simons, *What Katy Read*, 1995, p.2

Introduction

1   Beverly Lyon Clark, *Regendering the School Story*, Garland Publishing Co., 1996, p.7

2   Anne W. Ellis, *The Family Story in the 1960s*, Bingley, 1970, p.15

3   Chambers were reluctant to continue the Chalet series after *Jo Returns to the Chalet School*, because 'there are now twelve and that is enough'. See Helen McClelland, *Behind the Chalet School*, 2nd ed. 1996, p.224

4   As Enid Blyton did with her St Clare's and Malory Towers girls.

5   *Chaletian* 8 (1994), p.19

6   Dennis L. Bird, 'Nancy Calls the Tune: Some Reflections'. *Serendipity* 1 (1994), p.9

7   Polly Goerres, 'Excitements for the Chalet Fans'. In Rosemary Auchmuty and Juliet Gosling, eds., *The Chalet School Revisited*, 1994, p.92

8   DFB, *Dimsie Goes Back*, 1927

9   See, for example, EMB-D, *A Chalet Girl from Kenya,* 1955, p.154; but there are many instances of this.

10   For the addresses of the appreciation societies and the fanzines, see the Bibliography.

11   Girls' series books in the USA, for instance, have both well-developed collectors' networks and resources and, more recently, a growing body of feminist scholarship. See, for example, The Society of Phantom Friends, *The Girls' Series Companion*, Rheem Valley, CA: SynSine Press, 1997 ed.; and Sherrie A. Inness, ed., *Nancy Drew and Company: Culture, Gender, and Girls' Series*, Bowling Green, OH: Bowling Green State University Popular Press, 1997

12   See Eva Löfgren, *Schoolmates of the Long-Ago*, 1993, pp.101–2

13   See Sue Sims, 'The Series Factor'. In Auchmuty and Gosling, eds., *The Chalet School Revisited,* 1994, pp.253–82

14   Anne Thompson, 'Coming Home', *Chaletian* 3 (1992), p.12

15   See note 12

16   Bridget Fowler, *The Alienated Reader*, 1991, p.1

17   J. S. Bratton, *The Impact of Victorian Children's Fiction*, 1981

18   Judith Rowbotham, *Good Girls Make Good Wives*, 1989

19   Kimberley Reynolds, *Girls Only?*, 1990

20   Ibid, p.98

21   Rowbotham, *Good Girls Make Good Wives*, p.10

22   Ibid, p.9

23   Adrienne Rich, 'Compulsory Heterosexuality and Lesbian Existence' (1980). In *Blood, Bread and Poetry*, 1986, pp.23–75

24   Reynolds, *Girls Only?*, p.14

25   Pamela Knights, 'Refashioning Girlhood? Little Women

in Lois Lowry and Louisa May Alcott'. *New Comparisons* 20 (1995), pp.146, 152

26 Isabel Quigly, *The Heirs of Tom Brown*, Oxford University Press, 1984, p.212

27 McClelland, *Behind the Chalet School*, p.2

28 Martin Spence, 'Video Killed the Radio Stars'. *Folly* 7 (1992), p.26

29 Njeri Fuller, 'Fixing Nancy Drew: African American Strategies for Reading'. In Carolyn Stewart Dyer and Nancy Tillman Romalov, *Rediscovering Nancy Drew*, University of Iowa Press, 1995, p.138

30 McClelland, *Behind the Chalet School*, p.194

1 Young and Free

1 Ruth Hall, *Dear Dr Stopes: Sex in the 1920s*, Penguin, 1981. On women's position in this period, see Ruth Adam, *A Woman's Place 1910–1975*, Chatto & Windus, 1975; Deirdre Beddoe, *Back to Home and Duty*, 1989; Diana Gittins, *Fair Sex: Family Size and Structure 1900–1939*, Hutchinson, 1982; Winifred Holtby, *Women and a Changing Civilization*, John Lane, The Bodley Head, 1934; Sheila Jeffreys, *The Spinster and her Enemies*, 1985; Jane Lewis, *Women in England 1870–1950: Sexual Divisions and Social Change*, Wheatsheaf, 1984

2 See Mary Cadogan, *And Then Their Hearts Stood Still*, 1994

3 Lynette Muir, 'Fifty Years of the Hamlet Club'. *Junior Bookshelf* 30/1 (1966), p.23

4 DFB, *Nancy in the Sixth*, 1935, p.88

5 EJO, *The Abbey Girls on Trial*, 1931

6 EMB-D, *The School at the Chalet*, 1925

7 DFB, *The Serendipity Shop*, 1947, p.23

8 Ibid, p.99

9 Virginia Woolf, *A Room of One's Own*, Hogarth Press, 1928; Hilary Bailey, *Vera Brittain*, Penguin, 1987, pp.51–3

10   In EJO, *The Abbey Girls Go Back to School*, 1922, and *The Abbey Girls in Town*, 1925

11   EJO, *The Abbey Girls Go Back to School*, 1922, p.11

12   DFB, *Captain at Springdale*, 1932, p.9

13   EJO, *Rachel in the Abbey*, 1951, p.77

14   EMB-D, *Bride Leads the Chalet School*, 1953, p.9

15   See, for example, Catherine Sinclair, *Jane Bouverie, and How She Became an Old Maid*, Simpkin, Marshall & Co., 1855; Anon, *The Romance of a Dull Life*, Longman, 1861; and a twentieth-century example, Radclyffe Hall's depressing *The Unlit Lamp*, Cassell, 1924

16   See, for example, Nicholas Tucker, *The Child and the Book: A Psychological and Literary Exploration*, Cambridge University Press, 1981

17   EJO, *The New Abbey Girls*, 1923, p.98

18   EJO, *The Abbey Girls Again*, 1924, p.26

19   EJO, *Biddy's Secret*, 1932, p.69

20   EJO, *The Abbey Girls Go Back to School*, 1922

21   EJO, *The Abbey Girls Again*, 1924, p.106

22   Joan's youth is dealt with in *The Abbey Girls*, 1920, and in the retrospective novels from *Schooldays at the Abbey*, 1938, to *Tomboys at the Abbey*, 1957

23   EJO, *The Abbey Girls in Town*, 1925, p.261

24   EJO, *The New Abbey Girls*, 1923, p.71

25   EJO, *The Abbey Girls on Trial*, 1931, p.261

26   Ibid, pp.63, 67

27   Ibid, pp.70, 111

28   EJO, *Rosamund's Victory*, 1933, p.256

29   EJO, *Maidlin Bears the Torch*, 1937, p.70

30   Sheila Ray and Stella Waring, *EJO: Her Work*, rev. ed. 1997, p.60

31   EJO, *Biddy's Secret*, 1932, p.68

32   Ibid, p.81

33   EMB-D, *The Rivals of the Chalet School*, 1929, p.31

34   EMB-D, *The Chalet Girls in Camp*, 1932, p.165

35 EMB–D, *The New House at the Chalet School*, 1935, p.29

36 Ibid, p.244

37 Ibid, p.29

38 EMB–D, *Jo Returns to the Chalet School*, 1936, p.91

39 EMB–D, *The New Chalet School*, 1938, p.294

40 EJO, *The Abbey Girls on Trial*, 1931, Chapter 17, and *The New Abbey Girls*, 1923, Chapters 7 and 20

41 DFB, *The Serendipity Shop*, 1947, and *The Bartle Bequest*, 1955

42 M.V. Hughes, *A London Home of the 1890s*, Oxford University Press, 1946, p.28

43 EJO, *The Troubles of Tazy*, 1926, p.20

44 Ibid, pp.62–3

45 Bill Birkett and Bill Peascod, *Women Climbing: 200 Years of Achievement*, A & C Black, 1989, p.18

46 Ibid, p.23; and see Martin Spence, 'Women on the Rope'. New Chalet Club *Journal* 4 (1996), p.44

47 Ronald G. Clark, *The Alps*, Weidenfeld & Nicolson, 1973, Chapter 12; Piers Brendon, *Thomas Cook: 150 Years of Popular Tourism*, Secker & Warburg, 1991, Chapter 5

48 *Miss Jemima's Swiss Journal*, Putnam, 1962 (1863)

49 Arnold Lunn, *Switzerland and the English*, Eyre & Spottiswoode, 1944, p.133

50 Ibid, p.151

51 Maria Aitken, *'A Girdle Round the Earth': Women Travellers and Adventurers*, Robinson Publishing, 1988, p.13

52 Virginia Woolf, *Three Guineas*, 1938; Penguin ed. 1977, p.188

53 Shirley Angell, *Pinnacle Club: A History of Women Climbing*, The Pinnacle Club, 1988

54 Rosemary Auchmuty, *A World of Girls*, 1992, pp.59–64

55 EJO, *The Two Form-Captains*, 1921, p.128

56 Dorothy Watson, *Their Own Worst Enemies*, 1995, p.1

57 Ibid, p.6

2 Love and Marriage

1   EJO, *The Two Form-Captains*, 1921, p.270
2   EJO, *The Abbey Girls Again*, 1924, p.113
3   Adrienne Rich, 'Compulsory Heterosexuality and Lesbian Existence'. In *Blood, Bread, and Poetry*, 1987, pp.23–75
4   EMB-D, *The Maids of La Rochelle*, 1924, p.141
5   EJO, *Queen of the Abbey Girls*, 1926, p.169
6   EJO, *Queen of the Abbey Girls*, 1926
7   EJO, *Maid of the Abbey*, 1943
8   EJO, *Two Queens at the Abbey*, 1959
9   DFB, *Dimsie Grows Up*, 1924
10   EJO, *Rosamund's Victory*, 1933
11   EJO, *Selma at the Abbey*, 1952, pp.121, 195
12   Mary Cadogan and Patricia Craig, *You're a Brick, Angela!*, 1976, pp.192–3
13   Mary Cadogan, *And Then Their Hearts Stood Still*, 1994, p.310
14   Jay Dixon, *The Romantic Fiction of Mills & Boon, 1909–1990s*, UCL Press, 1999
15   Eva Löfgren, *Schoolmates of the Long-Ago*, 1993, p.38
16   EJO, *The Abbey Girls in Town*, 1925, p.173
17   DFB, *Dimsie Goes Back*, 1927, pp.274–5
18   EMB-D, *The Chalet School Goes to It*, 1941, p.154
19   EMB-D, *Jo to the Rescue*, 1945, p.196
20   EJO, *The Abbey Girls in Town*, 1925
21   DFB, *Dimsie Grows Up*, 1924
22   EMB-D, *The Chalet School and Jo*, 1931
23   DFB, *Nancy Calls the Tune*, 1944
24   EJO, *The Abbey Girls Go Back to School*, 1922, p.234
25   EJO, *The Girl Who Wouldn't Make Friends*, 1909, p.152
26   EMB-D, *Janie of La Rochelle*, 1932, p.111
27   Ibid, p.121
28   Helen McClelland, *Behind the Chalet School*, 2nd ed. 1996, p.200

29   EMB–D, *Adrienne and the Chalet School*, 1965, p.45

30   EMB–D, *A Problem for the Chalet School*, 1956, pp.145–6

31   DFB, *Dimsie Grows Up* (1924), 1st Australian ed. 1947, p.64

32   Ibid, p.68

33   Ibid, p.262

34   Ibid, p.228

35   DFB, *The Serendipity Shop*, 1947, pp.180–1

36   Cadogan, *And Then Their Hearts Stood Still*, p.274

37   EJO, *Queen of the Abbey Girls*, 1926, Chapter 9

38   EJO, *Joy's New Adventure*, 1935, p.177

39   Ibid, p.225

40   EJO, *Maidlin Bears the Torch*, 1937, p.236. (And see EJO, *Joy's New Adventure*, 1935, p.52, where Jen says: 'Poor Rosie! ... why should she give up her life to nursing men?')

41   Ibid, pp.244–5

42   Sheila Ray, '"Wide Shimmering Firth": The Colmskirk Novels of Dorita Fairlie Bruce', *Serendipity* 5 (1996), p.13

43   DFB, *Wild Goose Quest*, 1945, p.126

44   Ibid, p.150

45   Ibid, p.165

46   Ibid, p.166

47   Ibid, p.167

48   Shereen Benjamin, '"Doing Girl": Alternative Fantasies and Fictions in Girls' School Stories'. *New Chalet Club Journal* 11 (1998), p.35

49   EJO, *The Abbey Girls in Town*, 1925, p.259

50   EJO, *Queen of the Abbey Girls*, 1926, p.185

51   Ibid, p.209

52   See Rosemary Auchmuty, *A World of Girls*, 1992, pp.174–7

53   DFB, *Prefects at Springdale*, 1936, p.32

54   Ibid, p.282

55   DFB, *Dimsie Carries On* (1941), 1st Australian ed. 1946, p.163

56   DFB, *The Bartle Bequest*, 1955, p.251

57   Bridget Fowler, *The Alienated Reader*, 1991, p.54

58   EMB-D, *The Head Girl of the Chalet School*, 1928, p.181

59   DFB, *Dimsie, Head Girl* (1925), Australian ed. n.d., p.234

60   EJO, *Guardians of the Abbey*, 1950, p.137

61   EJO, *Maid of the Abbey*, 1943, p.144

62   Fiona Cownie with Joy Wotton, '"A Solid Lump of
      Comfort": Marriage in the Chalet School', and Jill
      Eckersley, 'Joey Maynard – The First Superwoman?' Both
      in Joy Wotton, ed., New Chalet Club *Journal* Supplement
      No 3 (1997), pp.1–11, and pp.26–30

63   McClelland, *Behind the Chalet School*, p.174; see also
      pp.248–9

64   EJO, *Maidlin Bears the Torch*, 1937, p.131

65   EJO, *Joy's New Adventure*, 1935, p.163

66   EJO, *Maidlin Bears the Torch*, 1937, p.181

67   Ibid, p.131

68   EJO, *Two Joans at the Abbey*, 1945, p.33

69   EJO, *An Abbey Champion*, 1946, p.22

70   Ibid, pp.72, 70

71   EJO, *Queen of the Abbey Girls*, 1926, p.95

72   EJO, *The Abbey Girls Again*, 1924, p.234

73   EJO, *The Secrets of Vairy*, 1947, pp.28–9

74   EJO, *Maidlin Bears the Torch*, 1937, pp.178–9

75   Ibid, p.179

76   EMB-D, *Gay from China at the Chalet School*, 1944, p.119

77   EMB-D, *The School at the Chalet*, 1925, p.12

78   DFB, *Nancy Calls the Tune*, 1944, p.30

79   EJO, *Robins in the Abbey*, 1947

80   Judith Rowbotham, *Good Girls Make Good Wives*, 1989,
      pp.45–6

81   EJO, *Maidlin Bears the Torch*, 1937, p.239

82   Löfgren, *Schoolmates of the Long-Ago*, p.137

83   DFB, *Captain at Springdale*, 1932, p.212

84   Ibid, p.211

85   DFB, *Dimsie Carries On* (1941), 1st Australian ed. 1946, pp.167–8

86   EMB-D, *Jo to the Rescue*, 1945, p.55

87   EMB-D, *Janie Steps In*, 1953, p.245. And see Jack Maynard at the breakfast table handing out the mail (*The Chalet School Triplets*, 1963, p.171) and the money (*A Chalet Girl from Kenya*, 1955, p.17).

88   EMB-D, *Janie of La Rochelle*, 1932, p.93

89   DFB, *Wild Goose Quest*, 1945, p.125

90   DFB, *The New House-Captain*, 1928

91   EMB-D, *The Chalet School and Jo*, 1931, p.22

92   EMB-D, *Bride Leads the Chalet School*, 1953, p.9

93   EJO, *A Fiddler for the Abbey*, 1948, pp.7, 15

94   EJO, *Strangers at the Abbey*, 1951, p.58

95   EJO, *Queen of the Abbey Girls*, 1926, p.54

96   EJO, *Schoolgirl Jen at the Abbey*, 1950, p.232

97   EJO, *The Abbey Girls Again*, 1924, p.301

98   EJO, *Queen of the Abbey Girls*, 1926, p.274

99   DFB, *Dimsie Carries On* (1941), 1st Australian ed. 1946, pp.46, 32–3

100 EJO, *Goblin Island*, 1907, p.53

101 EJO, *New Girls at Wood End*, 1957, p.137

102 EJO, *Two Joans at the Abbey*, 1945, p.22

103 EJO, *Rachel in the Abbey*, 1951, p.174

104 EJO, *A Fiddler for the Abbey*, 1948, p.16

105 Cadogan and Craig, *You're a Brick, Angela!*, p.174

106 McClelland, *Elinor M. Brent-Dyer's Chalet School*, 1989, p.50

107 EMB-D, *Joey Goes to the Oberland*, 1954, p.26

108 EMB-D, *Jo to the Rescue*, 1945, p.203

109 Ibid, p.205

110 EMB-D, *Lorna at Wynyards*, 1947, p.152

111 EMB-D, *Shocks for the Chalet School*, 1952, p.16

112 EMB-D, *Jo to the Rescue*, 1945, pp.83–4

113 EMB–D, *The Highland Twins at the Chalet School*, 1942, pp.59–60

114 Eckersley, 'Joey Maynard – The First Superwoman?', p.29

115 EMB–D, *Jo to the Rescue*, 1945, p.79

116 EMB–D, *Janie Steps In*, 1953, p.17

117 EJO, *Rosamund's Victory*, 1933, p.113

118 EJO, *The Troubles of Tazy*, 1926, pp.285–6

119 EMB–D, *Jean of Storms* (1930), 1996, p.17

120 EJO, *Biddy's Secret*, 1932, pp.219–20

121 Ibid p.101

122 *The Abbey Chronicle* 5 (1990), p.11

123 EJO, *The Abbey Girls Play Up*, 1930, p.159

3 Old Maids

1 DFB, *Triffeny*, 1950, pp.19–20

2 Ibid, p.173

3 Ibid, p.123

4 Ibid, p.25

5 Barbara Macdonald, *Look Me in the Eye*, 1983, p.73

6 Cynthia Rich, 'Aging, Ageism and Feminist Avoidance'. In Macdonald, *Look Me in the Eye*, p.55

7 For example, Florence Nightingale. See her *Suggestions for Thought to Searchers after Religious Truth*, 1860, Vol. II, pp.58–9

8 H. Lawrenny, 'Custom and Sex'. *Fortnightly Review* New Series XI (1872), p.311

9 *Population Trends* 48 (1987), pp.14–15

10 Lilian M. Faithfull, *In the House of My Pilgrimage*, 1924, p.63

11 Deirdre Beddoe, *Back to Home and Duty*, 1989, p.8

12 See Rosemary Auchmuty, *A World of Girls*, 1992, p.143

13 *Population Trends* 48 (1987), p.14

14 EMB–D, *The Chalet School Goes to It*, 1941, p.247

15 Laura Hutton, *The Single Woman and her Emotional Problems*, Ballière, Tindall and Cox, 1935, p.7

16 DFB, *Nancy Returns to St Bride's*, 1938, p.262

17 Hutton, *The Single Woman and her Emotional Problems*, pp.56–7

18 Leonora Eyles, *Unmarried but Happy*, Victor Gollancz, 1947, pp.41, 46

19 Auchmuty, 'The Chalet School Guides: Girls' Organisations and Girls' School Stories'. In Rosemary Auchmuty and Juliet Gosling, eds., *The Chalet School Revisited*, 1994, pp.173–212

20 M. B. Smith, *The Single Woman of Today: Her Problems and Adjustment*, Watts & Co., 1951, p.vii

21 EMB-D, *The Chalet School and Jo*, 1931, p.190

22 DFB, *Triffeny*, 1950, p.1

23 Ibid, p.4

24 DFB, *The Debatable Mound*, 1953, p.232

25 EMB-D, *Gay from China at the Chalet School*, 1944, p.126

26 EMB-D, *Chudleigh Hold*, 1954, p.89

27 Ibid, p.106

28 Ibid, pp.108–9

29 Ibid, p.109

30 Ibid, pp.135–6

31 Ibid, p.138

32 Ibid, p.204

33 Ibid, p.203

34 Ibid, pp.113–14

35 EMB-D, *Top Secret*, 1955, p.89

36 Ibid, p.90

37 Macdonald, *Look Me in the Eye*, p.92

38 EMB-D, *Kennelmaid Nan*, 1954, p.38

39 DFB, *Dimsie Carries On*, (1941) 1st Australian ed. 1946, p.213

40 DFB, *Dimsie Among the Prefects*, 1923, Australian ed. p.127

41 Miss Nalder, Miss Carey and Miss Norton

42   EMB-D, *Challenge for the Chalet School*, 1966, p.11

43   Chalet Club *News Letter* 11 (1964), p.2

44   EMB-D, *Gay from China at the Chalet School*, 1944, p.122

45   Auchmuty, *A World of Girls*, pp.126–33

46   EMB-D, *Challenge for the Chalet School*, 1966, p.58

47   Ibid, p.78

48   EMB-D, *The Chalet School Reunion*, 1963, pp.15–16

49   Mary Evans, *A Good School: Life at a Girl's Grammar School in the 1950s*, The Women's Press, 1991, p.60

50   Alison Hennegan in Liz Heron, ed., *Truth, Dare or Promise*, 1985, p.148

51   Julia Pascal ibid, p.41

52   Judith Humphrey, 'My God, It's the Head!'. In Auchmuty and Gosling, eds., *The Chalet School Revisited*, p.236

53   EMB-D, *The New Mistress at the Chalet School*, 1957, p.43

54   DFB, *Dimsie Goes to School [The Senior Prefect]*, 1920, p.21

55   Humphrey, 'My God, It's the Head!', p.215

56   DFB, *Dimsie Goes to School*, 1925, p.26 (first published as *The Senior Pefect*)

57   EMB-D, *The New Chalet School*, 1938, pp.205–6

58   Humphrey, 'My God, It's the Head!', p.243

59   EMB-D, *Gay from China at the Chalet School*, 1944, p.55

60   DFB, *The School in the Woods*, 1940, p.39

61   Ibid, pp.97–8

62   Ibid, p.40

63   Ibid, p.228

64   Auchmuty, *A World of Girls*, Chapter 6

65   EJO, *Goblin Island*, 1907, p.60

66   Ibid, p.228

67   Monica Godfrey, *Elsie Jeanette Oxenham and her Books*, 1979, p.6

68   EJO, *The Abbey Girls Go Back to School*, 1922, p.202

69   EJO, *An Abbey Champion*, 1946, p.135

70   EJO, *A Fiddler for the Abbey*, 1948, p.195

71   EJO, *The Abbey Girls on Trial*, 1931, p.110

72 EJO, *Biddy's Secret*, 1932, p.26

73 EJO, *Guardians of the Abbey*, 1950, p.136

74 Juliet Gosling, 'School with Bells On!'. In Auchmuty and Gosling, eds., *The Chalet School Revisited*, p.155

4 Community

1 EJO, *The Abbey Girls Again*, 1924, p.184

2 See EJO, *Adventure for Two*, 1941, p.19; *The Troubles of Tazy*, 1926, p.21; and *The New Abbey Girls*, 1923, p.86

3 EMB-D, *Lavender Laughs in the Chalet School*, 1943, p.152

4 Sheila Ray, 'The Literary Context'. In Rosemary Auchmuty and Juliet Gosling, eds., *The Chalet School Revisited*, 1994, p.112

5 Gillian Avery, *Childhood's Pattern: A Study of the Heroes and Heroines of Children's Fiction 1770–1950*, Hodder & Stoughton, 1975, p.228

6 Suzanne Neild and Rosalind Pearson, *Women Like Us*, The Women's Press, 1992, p.33

7 EJO, *The Troubles of Tazy*, 1926, pp.34–5

8 EJO, *The Abbey Girls on Trial*, 1931, pp.43, 65, 136, 139

9 EJO, *Maidlin to the Rescue*, 1934, pp.167–8

10 EJO, *Maidlin Bears the Torch*, 1937, p.241

11 EJO, *A Fiddler for the Abbey*, 1948, p.61

12 EMB-D, *Jo to the Rescue*, 1945, p.149

13 DFB, *Dimsie Grows Up* (1924), 1st Australian ed. 1947, p.281

14 Rosemary Auchmuty, *A World of Girls*, 1992, Chapter 5

15 For instance, DFB, *Dimsie Intervenes*, 1937, p.188

16 Malcolm Cole, *Whitelands College May Queen Festival 1881–1981*, Whitelands College Monographs, 1981

17 EJO, *The Abbey Girls Go Back to School*, 1922, p.10

18 EJO, *The Abbey Girls Again*, 1924, p.232

19 EJO, *Biddy's Secret*, 1932, p.31

20   EJO, *The Abbey Girls Go Back to School*, 1922, p.21

21   EJO, *A Fiddler for the Abbey*, 1948, p.170

22   EJO, *The Girls of the Hamlet Club*, 1914, p.182

23   Mary Cadogan and Patricia Craig, *You're a Brick, Angela!*, 1976, p. 163

24   For the history of the English Folk Dance Society, see Maud Karpeles, *Cecil Sharp: His Life and Work*, Routledge & Kegan Paul, 1967

25   Prunella Stack, *Movement is Life: An Autobiography*, Collins & Harvill Press, 1973, p.43

26   EJO, *The Abbey Girls in Town*, 1925

27   EJO, *The Abbey Girls Go Back to School*, 1922, p.104

28   Ibid, p.163

29   Florence Golding, 'What shall we wear?', *English Folk-Dance Society's Journal* 1/1 (May 1914), p.14

30   Karpeles, *Cecil Sharp*, p.83

31   EJO, *The Abbey Girls Again*, 1924, p.31

32   Douglas Kennedy, *English Folk Dancing: Today and Yesterday*, G. Bell & Sons, London, 1964, p.28

33   Ibid, pp. 7–8

34   Membership details are given in the EFDS *Annual Reports*. Elsie Oxenham's name appears in 1920 and is still there in 1938, the last volume to list members.

35   EJO, *The Abbey Girls Go Back to School*, 1922, p.77

36   EJO, *The Abbey Girls in Town*, 1925, p.114

37   EJO, *The Abbey Girls Go Back to School*, 1922, p.154

38   EJO, *The New Abbey Girls*, 1923, p.133

39   EJO, *The Abbey Girls Play Up*, 1930, pp.69–70

40   Monica Godfrey, *Elsie Jeanette Oxenham and her Books*, 1979, p.14

41   EJO, *The Abbey Girls at Home*, 1929, pp.191, 238

42   EJO, *An Abbey Champion*, 1946; *Robins in the Abbey*, 1947, p.163

43   Helen McClelland, *Behind the Chalet School*, 2nd ed. 1996, p.131

44 Ibid

45 Ibid, p.132

46 EMB-D, *The Maids of La Rochelle*, 1924, p.127

47 EMB-D, *Carnation of the Upper Fourth*, 1934, p.45

48 EMB-D, *Heather Leaves School*, 1929, p.29

49 McClelland, *Behind the Chalet School*, p.131

50 See Auchmuty, *A World of Girls*, pp.9–12

51 Cadogan and Craig, *You're a Brick, Angela!*, p.194

52 Godfrey, *Elsie Jeanette Oxenham and her Books*, p.14

53 EJO, *The Abbey Girls Again*, 1924, pp.164–5; EJO, *The New Abbey Girls*, 1923, p.233

54 EJO, *The Abbey Girls Go Back to School*, 1922, p.154

55 Auchmuty, *A World of Girls*, p.173

56 *The Book of the Camp Fire Girls*, 1922, p.21 (with Supplement for the British Isles)

57 Marion Lochhead, *A Lamp was Lit: The Girls' Guildry Through Fifty Years*, The Moray Press, 1949, p.25

58 Eva Löfgren, *Schoolmates of the Long-Ago*, 1993, pp.96–7

59 Rose Kerr, *The Story of the Girl Guides*, The Girl Guides Association, rev. ed. 1937, p.29

60 McClelland, *Behind the Chalet School*, p.175

61 Helen Buckler, Mary F. Fiedler and Martha F. Allen, eds., *Wo-He-Lo: The Story of Camp Fire Girls 1910–1960*, Camp Fire Girls, Inc., 1961, pp.22–3

62 See, for example, EJO, *The School of Ups and Downs*, 1918, p.156; *Patience Joan, Outsider*, 1922, pp.111–12 and illustration facing p.104; *The Crisis in Camp Keema*, 1928, pp.49, 187

63 Auchmuty, 'The Chalet School Guides: Girls' Organisations and Girls' School Stories'. In Auchmuty and Gosling, eds., *The Chalet School Revisited*, pp.173–212

64 Valerie Walkerdine, 'Dreams from an Ordinary Childhood'. In Liz Heron, ed., *Truth, Dare or Promise*, 1985, p.65

65 DFB, *Dimsie Intervenes*, 1937, p.14

5 Careers

1　See, for example, Joan Perkin, *Victorian Women*, John Murray, 1993 and Philippa Levine, *Victorian Feminism 1850–1900*, 1987

2　Jo Manton, *Elizabeth Garrett Anderson*, Methuen, 1965

3　Cecil Woodham-Smith, *Florence Nightingale 1820–1910*, Constable, 1950, p.77

4　For example, Vera Brittain, *Testament of Youth*, Victor Gollancz, 1933; and see Deirdre Beddoe, *Back to Home and Duty*, 1989

5　Margaret Fletcher, *O, Call Back Yesterday*, Shakespeare Head Press, 1939, p.51

6　Sara A. Burstall, *Prospect and Retrospect: 60 Years of Women's Education*, Longmans, 1933, p.232

7　DFB, *The Serendipity Shop*, 1947, p.17

8　Josephine Elder, *Exile for Annis*, Children's Press edition 1954 (1938), p.62. Elder, incidentally, was a GP.

9　Winifred Peck, *A Little Learning*, Faber, 1952, p.163

10　EJO, *The Abbey Girls Play Up*, 1930, p.47

11　EJO, *The Troubles of Tazy*, 1926, p.246

12　EJO, *Ven at Gregory's*, 1925, p.118

13　Ibid, p.45

14　Ibid, p.102

15　EJO, *The Troubles of Tazy*, 1926, p.11

16　Ibid, p.58

17　Ibid, p.298

18　Ibid, p.316

19　EJO, *An Abbey Champion*, 1946, p.159

20　DFB, *Dimsie Goes Back*, 1927, p.140

21　EMB-D, *Carnation of the Upper Fourth*, 1934, pp.90–1

22　EMB-D, *The Chalet School in the Oberland*, 1952, p.49

23　DFB, *Dimsie Goes Back*, 1925, p.209

24　Sheila Ray, '"Wide Shimmering Firth": The Colmskirk Novels of Dorita Fairlie Bruce'. *Serendipity* 5 (1996), p.12

25   EJO, *The Abbey Girls Play Up*, 1930, p.256

26   EJO, *The Junior Captain*, 1923, p.229

27   EJO, *The New Abbey Girls*, 1923, p.133

28   EJO, *The Abbey Girls Again*, 1924, pp.15, 27, 52

29   Ibid, p.13

30   EJO, *The Abbey Girls in Town*, 1925, p.12

31   EJO, *Maidlin to the Rescue*, 1934, Chapter XIV

32   Ibid, Chapter XVI

33   EJO, *Patience and Her Problems*, 1927, p.110

34   Ibid, p.300

35   EJO, *The Abbey Girls Win Through*, 1928

36   DFB, *Dimsie Moves Up Again* (1922), Australian ed. n.d., p.175

37   See Rita McWilliams-Tullberg, *Women at Cambridge*, Victor Gollancz, 1975

38   DFB, *Dimsie, Head Girl* (1925), Australian ed. n.d., p.188

39   DFB, *Dimsie Goes Back*, 1927, p.25

40   DFB, *Dimsie Grows Up* (1924), 1st Australian ed. 1947, p.67

41   DFB, *Dimsie, Head Girl*, 1925, and *Dimsie Carries On*, 1941

42   DFB, *Dimsie Grows Up*, 1924

43   DFB, *Sally Scatterbrain*, 1956, pp.20–1

44   DFB, *Dimsie Carries On* (1941), 1st Australian ed. 1946, p.53

45   Ibid, p.54

46   Mary Cadogan and Patricia Craig, *You're a Brick, Angela!*, 1976, p.186

47   Eva Löfgren, *Schoolmates of the Long-Ago*, 1993, p.120

48   DFB, *Toby at Tibbs Cross*, 1942; *Nancy Calls the Tune*, 1944. See Dennis L. Bird, '"Charity is Kind": A Character Study'. *Serendipity* 4 (1995), pp.9–14

49   EJO, *The School Torment*, 1920, pp.13, 10

50   EJO, *Strangers at the Abbey*, 1951, p.80

51   EMB-D, *Changes for the Chalet School*, 1953, pp.124–5

52 EMB–D, *The Chalet School and the Island*, 1950, p.155

53 EMB–D, *The New Mistress at the Chalet School*, 1957, Chapter 1

54 EMB–D, *The Princess of the Chalet School*, 1927, p.151

55 EMB–D, *The Chalet School and Richenda*, 1958, p.72

56 EMB–D, *Gay from China at the Chalet School*, 1944, p.122

57 Ibid, p.108

58 Löfgren, *Schoolmates of the Long-Ago*, pp.225–6

59 DFB, *Dimsie Goes Back*, 1927, p.274

60 Sarah M. Burn, 'Connections'. *Serendipity* 8 (1997), pp.14–16

61 EJO, *The Song of the Abbey*, 1954, p.172

62 EJO, *New Girls at Wood End*, 1957, p.126

63 EJO, *The New Abbey Girls*, 1923, p.258

64 EJO, *Tomboys at the Abbey*, 1957, p.211

65 Ibid, pp.212–13

66 See Elizabeth Wilson, *Only Halfway to Paradise*, 1980

67 *The Chalet Book for Girls*, 1947, p.111

68 Ibid, p.114

69 Ibid, p.111

70 Ibid, p.112

71 Ibid, p.114

72 Ray, '"Wide Shimmering Firth", p.13

73 DFB, *The Debatable Mound*, 1953, pp.5–9

74 DFB, *Sally Scatterbrain*, 1956, *Sally Again*, 1959, *Sally's Summer Term*, 1961

75 DFB, *The Debatable Mound*, 1953

76 DFB, *The Serendipity Shop*, 1947, pp.24, 169

77 DFB, *Nancy Returns to St Bride's*, 1938, p.52; *Dimsie Grows Up*, 1924

78 DFB, *Toby at Tibbs Cross*, 1942, p.7

79 *Serendipity* 7 (1996), pp.44–5

80 Rosamund Bertram, *Ann Thorne, Reporter*, (n.d., Nelson, and three sequels 1941–51

81 EMB–D, *Tom Tackles the Chalet School*, 1955, p.103

82 Alva Myrdal and Viola Klein, *Women's Two Roles: Home and Work*, Routledge & Kegan Paul, 2nd ed. 1968, pp.55–8

83 DFB, *The New Girl and Nancy*, 1926, p.288

84 EMB-D, *The New Mistress at the Chalet School*, 1957, Chapter 1

85 Mary Evans, *A Good School: Life at a Girls' Grammar School in the 1950s*, The Women's Press, 1991, p.38

Conclusion

1 Joseph McAleer, *Popular Reading and Publishing in Britain 1914–1950*, 1992, p.7

2 Ibid, p.143

3 See Deirdre Beddoe, *Back to Home and Duty*, 1989, especially Chapter 1

4 Brian Braithwaite and Joan Barrell, *The Business of Women's Magazines*, Kogan Page, 2nd ed. 1988, pp.26, 41–6. *Boyfriend* ran from 1959. Other magazines for teenage girls of the period included *Marilyn* (1955), *Honey* (1960), *Nineteen* (1961) and *Jackie* (1964).

5 Sheila Ray, '"Wide Shimmering Firth": The Colmskirk Novels of Dorita Fairlie Bruce'. *Serendipity* 5 (1996), p.13

6 Ibid, p.16

7 EMB-D, *Jo to the Rescue*, 1945, p.56

8 Eva Löfgren, *Schoolmates of the Long-Ago*, 1993, pp.102–3

9 Meg Crane, 'Thekla von Stift: the Case for the Defence'. Friends of the Chalet School *Newsletter* 27 (1995), pp.42–8; and 'Bill of the Chalet School'. Friends of the Chalet School *Newsletter* 33 (1996), pp.41–5, continued in subsequent issues.

10 Helen McClelland, *Behind the Chalet School*, 2nd ed. 1996, p.283

11 *Folly* 9 (1993), p.21

12   Joy Wotton, 'News of Old Girls', New Chalet Club *Journal* 8 (1997), p.11

13   See, for example, Merryn Williams, *The Chalet Girls Grow Up*, 1998

14   Bridget Fowler, *The Alienated Reader*, 1991, p.4

15   Shereen Benjamin, '"Doing Girl": Alternative Fantasies and Fictions in Girls' School Stories'. New Chalet Club *Journal* 11 (1998), p.37

Bibliography

Each author's books are listed in order of publication. I am grateful to Sue Sims, Ruth Allen, Monica Godfrey and Joy Wotton for the work that has gone into making these lists as correct and complete as possible. Books about each author follow the listing for that author, together with the names and addresses of societies and journals dedicated to her. Finally, there is a selection of the general secondary sources I found most useful for this study. Other references can be found in the Notes.

Elinor M. Brent–Dyer

Books by Elinor M. Brent–Dyer
Gerry Goes to School, Chambers, 1922
A Head Girl's Difficulties, Chambers, 1923
The Maids of La Rochelle, Chambers, 1924
The School at the Chalet, Chambers, 1925
Jo of the Chalet School, Chambers, 1926
The Princess of the Chalet School, Chambers, 1927
Seven Scamps Who Are Not All Boys, Chambers, 1927
A Thrilling Term at Janeways, Nelson, 1927
The Head Girl of the Chalet School, Chambers, 1928
The New House Mistress, Nelson, 1928
Judy the Guide, Nelson, 1928
The Rivals of the Chalet School, Chambers, 1929
Heather Leaves School, Chambers, 1929
The School by the River, Burns, Oates & Washbourne, 1930

Eustacia Goes to the Chalet School, Chambers, 1930
The Chalet School and Jo, Chambers, 1931
The Feud in the Fifth Remove, Girls' Own Paper Office, 1931
The Little Marie-Jose, Burns, Oates & Washbourne, 1932
Janie of La Rochelle, Chambers, 1932
The Chalet Girls in Camp, Chambers, 1932
The Exploits of the Chalet Girls, Chambers, 1933
Carnation of the Upper Fourth, Girls' Own Paper Office, 1934
The Chalet School and the Lintons, Chambers, 1934
Elizabeth the Gallant, Thornton Butterworth, 1935
The New House at the Chalet School, Chambers, 1935
Jo Returns to the Chalet School, Chambers, 1936
Monica Turns Up Trumps, Girls' Own Paper Office, 1936
Caroline the Second, Girls' Own Paper Office, 1937
They Both Liked Dogs, Girls' Own Paper Office, 1938
The New Chalet School, Chambers, 1938
The Chalet School in Exile, Chambers, 1940
The Chalet School Goes to It, Chambers, 1941
The Highland Twins at the Chalet School, Chambers, 1942
The Little Missus, Chambers, 1942
Lavender Laughs in the Chalet School, Chambers, 1943
Gay from China at the Chalet School, Chambers, 1944
Jo to the Rescue, Chambers, 1945
The Lost Staircase, Chambers, 1946
The Chalet Book for Girls, Chambers, 1947
Lorna at Wynyards, Lutterworth Press, 1947
Stepsisters for Lorna, Temple, 1948
The Second Chalet Book for Girls, Chambers, 1948
The Third Chalet Book for Girls, Chambers, 1949
Three Go to the Chalet School, Chambers, 1949
The Chalet School and the Island, Chambers, 1950
Peggy of the Chalet School, Chambers, 1950
Fardingales, Latimer House, 1950
Carola Storms the Chalet School, Chambers, 1951
The Chalet School and Rosalie, Chambers, 1951

Verena Visits New Zealand, Chambers, 1951
Bess on her Own in Canada, Chambers, 1951
Quintette in Queensland, Chambers, 1951
Sharlie's Kenya Diary, Chambers, 1951
The Wrong Chalet School, Chambers, 1952
Shocks for the Chalet School, Chambers, 1952
The Chalet School in the Oberland, Chambers, 1952
The Chalet Girls' Cook Book, Chambers, 1953
Bride Leads the Chalet School, Chambers, 1953
Changes for the Chalet School, Chambers, 1953
Janie Steps In, Chambers, 1953
The 'Susannah' Adventure, Chambers, 1953
Chudleigh Hold, Chambers, 1954
The Condor Crags Adventure, Chambers, 1954
Nesta Steps Out, Oliphants, 1954
Kennelmaid Nan, Lutterworth Press, 1954
Joey Goes to the Oberland, Chambers, 1954
The Chalet School and Barbara, Chambers, 1954
Tom Tackles the Chalet School, Chambers, 1955
The Chalet School Does It Again, Chambers, 1955
A Chalet Girl from Kenya, Chambers, 1955
Top Secret, Chambers, 1955
Beechy of the Harbour School, Oliphants, 1955
Leader in Spite of Herself, Oliphants, 1956
Mary-Lou of the Chalet School, Chambers, 1956
A Genius at the Chalet School, Chambers, 1956
A Problem for the Chalet School, Chambers, 1956
The New Mistress at the Chalet School, Chambers, 1957
Excitements for the Chalet School, Chambers, 1957
The Coming-of-Age of the Chalet School, Chambers, 1958
The Chalet School and Richenda, Chambers, 1958
Trials for the Chalet School, Chambers, 1959
Theodora and the Chalet School, Chambers, 1959
Joey and Co. in Tirol, Chambers, 1960
Ruey Richardson, Chaletian, Chambers, 1960

A Leader in the Chalet School, Chambers, 1961
The Chalet School Wins the Trick, Chambers, 1961
A Future Chalet School Girl, Chambers, 1962
The Feud in the Chalet School, Chambers, 1962
The School at Skelton Hall, Max Parrish, 1962
The Trouble at Skelton Hall, Max Parrish, 1963
The Chalet School Triplets, Chambers, 1963
The Chalet School Reunion, Chambers, 1963
Jane and the Chalet School, Chambers, 1964
Redheads at the Chalet School, Chambers, 1964
Adrienne and the Chalet School, Chambers, 1965
Summer Term at the Chalet School, Chambers, 1965
Challenge for the Chalet School, Chambers, 1966
Two Sams at the Chalet School, Chambers, 1967
Althea Joins the Chalet School, Chambers, 1969
Prefects of the Chalet School, Chambers, 1970
Jean of Storms (1930), Bettany Press, 1996

Secondary sources

Auchmuty, Rosemary and Juliet Gosling, eds. *The Chalet School Revisited*. London: Bettany Press, 1994

McClelland, Helen. *Behind the Chalet School*. Bognor: New Horizon, 1981; 2nd ed. London: Bettany Press, 1996

—— *The Chalet School Companion*. London: HarperCollins, 1994

—— *Elinor M. Brent-Dyer's Chalet School*. London: HarperCollins, 1989

—— *Visitors for the Chalet School*. London: Bettany Press, 1995 (reconstruction of a 'missing' Chalet School story).

Williams, Merryn. *The Chalet Girls Grow Up*. Wootton, Beds: Plas Gwyn Books, 1998 (continuation of the Chalet series).

Societies and journals

Chalet Club News Letters 1–20 (1959–60). Edinburgh: Chambers

Chaletian 1–9 (1991–4)

Friends of the Chalet School *Newsletter* (1989–). Ann Mackie-Hunter and Clarissa Cridland, 4 Rock Terrace, Coleford, Bath BA3 5NF

The New Chalet Club *Journal* (1995–). Helen Aveling, 1 Carpenter Court, Neath Hill, Milton Keynes MK14 6JP

Dorita Fairlie Bruce

Books by Dorita Fairlie Bruce
The Senior Prefect, OUP, 1921 (or 1920) (reissued as *Dimsie Goes to School*, 1925)
Dimsie Moves Up, OUP, 1921
Dimsie Moves Up Again, OUP, 1922
Dimsie Among the Prefects, OUP, 1923
The Girls of St Bride's, OUP, 1923
Dimsie Grows Up, OUP, 1924
Dimsie, Head Girl, OUP, 1925
That Boarding-School Girl, OUP, 1925
The New Girl and Nancy, OUP, 1926
Dimsie Goes Back, OUP, 1927
The New House-Captain, OUP, 1928
The Best House in the School, OUP, 1930
The King's Curate, John Murray, 1930
The School on the Moor, OUP, 1931
The Best Bat in the School, OUP, 1931
Captain at Springdale, OUP, 1932
Mistress Mariner, John Murray, 1932
Nancy at St Bride's, OUP, 1933
The New House at Springdale, OUP, 1934
Nancy in the Sixth, OUP, 1935
Prefects at Springdale, OUP, 1936
Dimsie Intervenes, OUP, 1937
Nancy to the Rescue, OUP, (1937)
Nancy Returns to St Bride's, OUP, 1938
Captain Anne, OUP, 1939
The School in the Woods, OUP, 1940
Dimsie Carries On, OUP, (1941)

Toby at Tibbs Cross, OUP, 1942

Nancy Calls the Tune, OUP, 1944

A Laverock Lilting, OUP, 1945

Wild Goose Quest, Lutterworth, 1945

The Serendipity Shop, OUP, 1947

Triffeny, OUP, 1950

The Bees on Drumwhinnie, OUP, 1952

The Debatable Mound, OUP, 1953

The Bartle Bequest, OUP, 1955

Sally Scatterbrain, Blackie, 1956

Sally Again, Blackie, 1959

Sally's Summer Term, Blackie, 1961

Secondary source

Löfgren, Eva Margareta. *Schoolmates of the Long-Ago: Motifs and Archetypes in Dorita Fairlie Bruce Boarding School Stories.* Stockholm: Symposion Graduate, 1993

Society/journal

Serendipity: The Magazine of the Dorita Fairlie Bruce Society (1994–). Carolyn Dedman, 3 Dudwell Cottages, Camrose, Haverfordwest, Pembrokeshire SA62 6HJ

Elsie J. Oxenham

Books by Elsie J. Oxenham

Goblin Island, Collins, 1907

A Princess in Tatters, Collins, 1908

The Conquest of Christina, Collins, 1909

The Girl Who Wouldn't Make Friends, Nelson, 1909

A Holiday Queen, Collins, 1910

Mistress Nanciebel, Hodder & Stoughton/OUP, 1910

Rosaly's New School, Chambers, 1913

Schoolgirls and Scouts, Collins, 1914

The Girls of the Hamlet Club, Collins, 1914

At School with the Roundheads, Chambers, 1915

Finding Her Family, SPCK, 1916

The Tuck-Shop Girl, Chambers, 1916

A School Camp Fire, Chamber, 1917

The School of Ups and Downs, Chambers, 1918

A Go-Ahead Schoolgirl, Chambers, 1919

Expelled from School, Collins, 1919

The Twins of Castle Charming, Swarthmore Press, 1920

The Abbey Girls, Collins, 1920

The School Torment, Chambers, 1920

The Two Form-Captains, Chambers, 1921

The Girls of the Abbey School, Collins, 1921

Patience Joan, Outsider, Cassell, 1922

The Captain of the Fifth, Chambers, 1922

The Abbey Girls Go Back to School, Collins, 1922

The New Abbey Girls, Collins, 1923

The Junior Captain, Chambers, 1923

Tickles; or, The School that was Different, Partridge, 1924

The School Without a Name, Chambers, 1924

The Abbey Girls Again, Collins, 1924

The Girls of Gwynfa, Warne, 1924

The Testing of the Torment, Cassell, 1925

Ven at Gregory's, Chambers, 1925

The Abbey Girls in Town, Collins, 1925

The Camp Fire Torment, Chambers, 1926

Queen of the Abbey Girls, Collins, 1926

The Troubles of Tazy, Chambers, 1926

Peggy Makes Good, RTS, 1927

Jen of the Abbey School, Collins, 1927 (reissued in three parts as *The Girls of Rocklands School*, 1929; *The Second Term at Rocklands*, 1930; *The Third Term at Rocklands*, 1931)

Patience and Her Problems, Chambers, 1927

The Crisis in Camp Keema, Chambers, 1928

The Abbey Girls Win Through, Collins, 1928

Deb at School, Chambers, 1929

The Abbey Girls at Home, Collins, 1929

Dorothy's Dilemma, Chambers, 1930

The Abbey Girls Play Up, Collins, 1930

Deb of Sea House, Chambers, 1934

The Abbey Girls on Trial, Collins, 1931 (first part reissued as *The Girls of Squirrel House*, 1932)

Biddy's Secret, Chambers, 1932

The Camp Mystery, Collins, 1932

Rosamund's Victory, Harrap, 1933

The Reformation of Jinty, Chambers, 1933

Maidlin to the Rescue, Chambers, 1934

Jinty's Patrol, Newnes, 1934

Joy's New Adventure, Chambers, 1935

Peggy and the Brotherhood, RTS, 1936

Rosamund's Tuckshop, RTS, 1937

Maidlin Bears the Torch, RTS, 1937

Sylvia of Sarn, Warne, 1937

Damaris at Dorothy's, SPCK, 1937

Rosamund's Castle, RTS, 1938

Schooldays at the Abbey, Collins, 1938

Secrets of the Abbey, Collins, 1939

Stowaways in the Abbey, Collins, 1940

Damaris Dances, OUP, 1940

Patch and a Pawn, Warne, 1940

Adventure for Two, OUP, 1941

Jandy Mac Comes Back, Collins, 1941

Pernel Wins, Frederick Muller, 1942

Maid of the Abbey, Collins, 1943

Elsa Puts Things Right, Frederick Muller, 1944

Daring Doranne, Frederick Muller, 1945

Two Joans at the Abbey, Collins, 1945

An Abbey Champion, Frederick Muller, 1946

Robins in the Abbey, Collins, 1947

The Secrets of Vairy, Frederick Muller, 1947

Margery Meets the Roses, Lutterworth Press, 1947

A Fiddler for the Abbey, Frederick Muller, 1948

Schoolgirl Jen at the Abbey, Collins, 1950

Guardians of the Abbey, Frederick Muller, 1950

Rachel in the Abbey, Frederick Muller, 1951

Strangers at the Abbey, Collins, 1951

Selma in the Abbey, Collins, 1952

A Dancer from the Abbey, Collins, 1953

The Song of the Abbey, Collins, 1954

New Girls at Wood End, Blackie, 1957

Tomboys at the Abbey, Collins, 1957

Two Queens at the Abbey, Collins, 1959

A Divided Patrol, Woodfield, 1992

Deb Leads the Dormitory, Woodfield, 1992

Secondary sources

Allen, Ruth. *The Books of Elsie J. Oxenham: A List in Reading Order*, 1997. Available from Ruth Allen, 32 Tadfield Road, Romsey, Hampshire SO51 5AJ

Godfrey, Monica, *Elsie Jeanette Oxenham and her Books*. London: Autolycus Publications, 1979

Muir, Lynette. 'Fifty Years of the Hamlet Club'. *Junior Bookshelf* 30/1 (1966), pp.19–23

Waring, Stella and Sheila Ray, *EJO: Her Work*. rev. ed. 1997 (1985)

Society/journal

The Abbey Chronicle: The Journal of the Elsie Jeanette Oxenham Appreciation Society (1989–). Ruth Allen, 32 Tadfield Road, Romsey, Hampshire SO51 5AJ

General

Auchmuty, Rosemary. *A World of Girls: The Appeal of the Girls' School Story*. London: The Women's Press, 1992

Avery, Gillian. *The Best Type of Girl: A History of Girls' Independent Schools*. London: André Deutsch, 1991

Beddoe, Deirdre. *Back to Home and Duty: Women Between the Wars 1918–1939*. London: Pandora, 1989

Bratton, J. S. *The Impact of Victorian Children's Fiction*. London: Croom Helm, 1981

Cadogan, Mary. *And Then Their Hearts Stood Still: An Exuberant Look at Romantic Fiction Past and Present*. London: Macmillan, 1994

—— *Chin Up, Chest Out, Jemina!: A Celebration of the Schoolgirl's Story*, Haslemere: Bonnington, 1989

Cadogan, Mary, and Patricia Craig. *You're a Brick, Angela!: A New Look at Girls' Fiction from 1839 to 1975*. London: Victor Gollancz, 1976; 2nd ed. (*to 1985*), 1986.

Crouch, Marcus. *The Nesbit Tradition: The Children's Novel in England, 1945–1970*. London: Ernest Benn, 1972

—— *Treasure Seekers and Borrowers: Children's Books in Britain 1900–1960*. London: Library Association, 1962

Foster, Shirley, and Judy Simons. *What Katy Read: Feminist Re-readings of 'Classic' Stories for Girls*. London: Macmillan, 1995

Fowler, Bridget. *The Alienated Reader: Women and Popular Romantic Literature in the Twentieth Century*. Hemel Hempstead: Harvester Wheatsheaf, 1991

Heron, Liz, ed. *Truth, Dare or Promise: Girls Growing Up in the Fifties.* London: Virago, 1985

Jeffreys, Sheila. *The Spinster and Her Enemies: Feminism and Sexuality 1880–1930*. London: Pandora, 1985

Levine, Philippa. *Victorian Feminism 1850–1900*. Oxford: Basil Blackwell, 1987

McAleer, Joseph. *Popular Reading and Publishing in Britain 1914-1950*. Oxford: Clarendon Press, 1992

Macdonald, Barbara, with Cynthia Rich. *Look Me in the Eye: Old Women, Aging and Ageism*. London: The Women's Press, 1983

Mitchell, Sally. *The New Girl: Girls' Culture in England, 1890-1915*. New York: Columbia University Press, 1995

Philips, Deborah, and Ian Haywood. *Brave New Causes: Women in British Postwar Fictions*. London: Leicester University Press, 1998

Ray, Sheila. 'School Stories'. In Peter Hunt, ed., *International Companion Encyclopaedia of Children's Literature*. London and New York: Routledge, 1996, pp. 348–59

Reynolds, Kimberley. *Girls Only? Gender and Popular Children's Fiction in Britain, 1880–1910*. Hemel Hempstead: Harvester Wheatsheaf, 1990

Rich, Adrienne. 'Compulsory Heterosexuality and Lesbian Existence' (1980). In *Blood, Bread and Poetry: Selected Prose 1979–1985*. London: Virago, 1986, pp.23–75

Rowbotham, Judith. *Good Girls Make Good Wives. Guidance for Girls in Victorian Fiction*. Oxford: Basil Blackwell, 1989

Tinkler, Penny. *Constructing Girlhood: Popular Magazines for Girls Growing Up in England 1920–1950*. London: Taylor & Francis, 1995

Trease, Geoffrey. *Tales Out of School*. London: New Education Book Club, 1948

Tucker, Nicholas. *The Child and the Book: A Psychological and Literary Exploration*. Cambridge University Press, 1981

Watson, Dorothy. *Their Own Worst Enemies: Women Writers of Women's Fiction*. London: Pluto, 1995

Wilson, Elizabeth. *Only Halfway to Paradise: Women in Postwar Britain 1945–1968*. London: Tavistock, 1980

Societies and journals

Children's Books History Society *Newsletter*. Mrs Pat Garrett, 25 Field Way, Hoddesdon, Herts EN11 0QN

Folly (Fans of Light Literature for the Young) (1990–). Sue Sims, 21 Warwick Road, Pokesdown, Bournemouth BH7 6JW